Bible Study Series
for senior high

Why Being a Christian Matters

Loveland, Colorado

Why Being a Christian Matters
Core Belief Bible Study Series

Copyright © 1997 Group Publishing, Inc.

All rights reserved. No part of this book may be reproduced in any manner whatsoever without prior written permission from the publisher, except where noted in the text and in the case of brief quotations embodied in critical articles and reviews. For information, write Permissions, Group Publishing, Inc., Dept. PD, P.O. Box 481, Loveland, CO 80539.

Credits
Editor: Karl Leuthauser
Managing Editor: Michael D. Warden
Chief Creative Officer: Joani Schultz
Copy Editor: Julie Meiklejohn
Art Director: Lisa Chandler
Cover Art Director: Helen H. Lannis
Cover Designer/Assistant Art Director: Bill Fisher
Computer Graphic Artist: Ray Tollison
Photographer: Craig DeMartino
Production Manager: Gingar Kunkel

Unless otherwise noted, Scriptures quoted from The Youth Bible, New Century Version, copyright © 1991 by Word Publishing, Dallas, Texas 75039. Used by permission.

ISBN 0-7644-0883-6

10 9 8 7 6 5 4 3 2   06 05 04 03 02 01 00 99 98 97

Printed in the United States of America.

Bible Study Series
for senior high

contents:

the Core Belief: ▼Salvation

It's a basic tenet of Christianity. Without it, we can have no relationship with God, because he is holy and we are sinful. But through his grace, God freely offered his holy Son as the sacrifice for our sin. Jesus Christ laid down his life and rose from the grave so that we could live forever.

As students participate in studies of this Core Christian Belief, they should discover that salvation can be theirs if they believe in Jesus Christ, turn away from their sin, and have faith that Jesus has their present circumstances as well as their eternal well-being in his hands. Jesus redeems us, frees us from the powers of sin and death, and renews us in him.

the ▼Helpful Stuff

SALVATION AS A CORE CHRISTIAN BELIEF **7**
(or How to Get a Clean Slate)

ABOUT CORE BELIEF BIBLE STUDY SERIES **10**
(or How to Move Mountains in One Hour or Less)

WHY ACTIVE AND INTERACTIVE LEARNING WORKS WITH TEENAGERS **55**
(or How to Keep Your Kids Awake)

YOUR EVALUATION **61**
(or How You Can Edit Our Stuff Without Getting Paid)

the Studies

Grave Concerns — 15
THE ISSUE: Death
THE BIBLE CONNECTION: John 1:12; Ephesians 2:4-5a, 8-9; Hebrews 2:14-18; and 1 John 5:11-13
THE POINT: Jesus defeated death for you.

Cult Repellent — 25
THE ISSUE: Cults
THE BIBLE CONNECTION: Matthew 7:15-23; John 14:6-7; and 1 Timothy 2:5-6
THE POINT: Faith in Jesus is the only way to eternal life.

Running on Empty — 35
THE ISSUE: Grace
THE BIBLE CONNECTION: John 1:14, 16-17; Romans 8:10-13; Ephesians 2:4-9; and Philippians 3:3-11
THE POINT: Life is empty without Jesus.

Like a Child — 45
THE ISSUE: Faith
THE BIBLE CONNECTION: Deuteronomy 1:31; Isaiah 43:1-7; Matthew 6:31-34; 11:25-30; 18:1-5; Romans 1:17; 8:14-17; Hebrews 11:1; and 1 John 3:1-2
THE POINT: Faith is simple trust in God.

Salvation as a Core Christian Belief

The goal of nearly every religion is for its followers to have a joyous afterlife. In most religions, that means hard work and suffering during life on earth as followers strive to attain a level of spirituality that assures their "salvation." However, God tells us that we must be perfect to live with him in heaven. And there's no way we can attain perfection on our own. No matter how hard we try to be good, we'll always fall short of God's perfect standard. That leaves us destined for an eternity of separation from God.

That's where the good news of God's salvation comes in! God loves us so much that long before any of us turned to him, he gave his own Son to suffer and die an agonizing death so that our sins could be forgiven. Then Jesus rose from the dead, defeating death for us so that we can live eternally with him—starting on the day we ask forgiveness for our sins and trust Jesus with our lives.

But do your kids know and live by this good news? In today's culture, your young people have exposure to all kinds of religions that proclaim different works that will gain people salvation, such as praying five times a day, meditating for hours, or cleansing themselves in a river. The performance orientation of our society further seduces young people into thinking they must do good works in order to be saved. Other young people don't even know they're lost. The "I'm OK, You're OK" mentality blinds them to their deepest need.

In *Why Being a Christian Matters,* your students will have the opportunity to uncover the folly of these false philosophies and theologies by looking at the reality of salvation through Jesus Christ. As you take them through the first study, kids will be challenged to understand that Jesus has won the victory over **death.** They can discover the certainty of their salvation in Jesus Christ. They can know that they have no reason for fear as long as they are living in him.

In the second study, students will be challenged to evaluate different "paths" to heaven. Kids will be given the tools to determine whether the path to heaven that is set before them is through Jesus Christ or through manipulative and damaging tactics offered by many **cults.** As they investigate, they can see that faith in Jesus is the only way to eternal life.

In the third study, students will have the opportunity to discover that salvation can't be earned or purchased. They can find that God's **grace** is a gift that will change their immediate and eternal circumstances. They can see that life is as abundant and fulfilled *within* God's grace as it is empty and purposeless *without* Jesus.

In the final study, kids will investigate one of the great mysteries of salvation—it comes to us through childlike **faith.** Your kids will be encouraged to hold on to a faith that requires nothing but simple trust in God.

Most people who accept God's gift of eternal life do so before they turn twenty, so the teenage years are vitally important to your kids' lives. Finding God's salvation now will not only empower your young people to live powerful, productive lives for God, it will also prevent them from wasting years in which they could've known a God who loves them more than life.

For a more comprehensive look at this Core Christian Belief, read Group's ***Get Real: Making Core Christian Beliefs Relevant to Teenagers.***

DEPTHFINDER — HOW THE BIBLE DESCRIBES SALVATION

To help you effectively guide your kids toward this Core Christian Belief, use these overviews as a launching point for a more in-depth study of salvation.

- **Grace.** No human being deserves eternal life with God. We all have sinned and can't possibly make ourselves good enough for God. That's where God's grace comes in. Grace is one element of God's unmerited favor. Only because of his grace toward us are any of us able to have relationship with him in any way. God, in his grace, has not only provided the way of salvation for us, but also strengthens us to continue following him (Romans 3:23-24; 5:15-17; Ephesians 2:8-9; Titus 2:11-14; and 1 Peter 5:10-12).

- **Repentance.** To repent is more than to feel sorry about something. Repentance is making a conscious decision to turn away from sinful attitudes and actions and move toward a life guided by the Holy Spirit. True repentance results in a changed life. Repentance involves both human and divine action. When the Holy Spirit prompts us to turn from our sin, God wants us to respond in faith by embracing the grace he offers. True faith is impossible without repentance, and true repentance is impossible without faith (Matthew 4:17; Luke 24:46-47; Acts 2:38; 3:19-21; 20:21; and 2 Peter 3:9).

- **Faith.** More than simple belief in Jesus' existence, faith is trusting Jesus fully for both our present circumstances and our eternal destiny. It means believing and accepting his teachings as well as personally trusting in the miracle of his death and resurrection. When we place our faith in God, we make a conscious decision to believe and to act on that belief—but it is a decision we could not make unless the Holy Spirit prompts us to do so (Romans 4:4-5; 10:17; Ephesians 2:8-9; Hebrews 11:6; and James 2:18-19).

- **Regeneration.** Related to the idea of being "born again," regeneration is the spiritual change in a human heart brought about by God's direct action. Through regeneration, our sinful spirits are reborn and made one with Christ. This change gives us the power to say no to sin. As Jesus came to life again after his crucifixion, we too have a new life in him. We become new creations, no longer slaves to sin but free to serve God faithfully (John 1:12-13; 3:3-8; 2 Corinthians 5:17; Ephesians 2:4-6; Titus 3:3-7; and 1 John 5:1).

- **Adoption.** Under Roman law, an adopted child had all the benefits of his or her new adoptive family but none of the debts or obligations of his or her natural family. In

Helpful Stuff   8

the same way, those who believe in Jesus are adopted as children of God and are freed from the debt of sin they owe. God adopts us as his children as an act of grace and love, giving us the privilege of becoming coheirs with Christ (John 1:12; Romans 8:5-17; Galatians 4:1-7; Ephesians 1:4-6; and 1 John 3:1-3).

- **Justification.** Because of what Jesus did in bearing our sins on the cross, God can declare us righteous before him. God's justice was satisfied at the cross because Jesus' death paid the penalty for our sins. Justification is more than forgiveness; it means erasing all record of the sin ever occurring (Romans 3:21-30; 5:1-2, 6-11, 15-19; 2 Corinthians 5:21; Galatians 3:6-8; and Philippians 3:7-9).

- **Redemption.** Redemption refers to Christ's loving choice to pay our debt. The Greek word for "redeemed" was one that today might be stamped on a receipt, indicating "paid in full." The price for our sin was beyond our ability to pay. We were bound for eternal death because of the unpaid bill. But in taking our sins with him to death on the cross, Jesus paid our bill in full. Through faith in Jesus, we're freed from the debt of sin. Redemption also carries with it a "freed to" component. We're freed *from* sin and death *to* new life in Christ, as if we actually died with him and rose again as he did. So Christ's redemptive act on the cross not only saves us from death but continues to work in us daily, transforming us to be more like Jesus (Mark 10:45; Romans 6:4; Ephesians 1:7-8; Colossians 1:13-14; 1 Peter 1:17-21; and 3:18).

- **Sanctification.** "Sanctified" means "set apart." Thus sanctification is being set apart for God's service. It's the primary work of the Holy Spirit in the Christian's life. Some believe that sanctification is a one-time experience in which a person can receive complete sanctification in an instant. Others believe it's a process through which we gradually become more holy through spiritual growth over many years. Whichever is the case, sanctification involves an intimate communion between the Holy Spirit's work in our lives and our faithful, obedient response to him (Romans 7:15-25; 1 Corinthians 6:9-11; 2 Corinthians 3:18; Philippians 2:12-13; and 2 Peter 1:3-9).

CORE CHRISTIAN BELIEF OVERVIEW

Here are the twenty-four Core Christian Belief categories that form the backbone of Core Belief Bible Study Series:

The Nature of God	Jesus Christ	The Holy Spirit
Humanity	Evil	Suffering
Creation	The Spiritual Realm	The Bible
Salvation	Spiritual Growth	Personal Character
God's Justice	Sin & Forgiveness	The Last Days
Love	The Church	Worship
Authority	Prayer	Family
Service	Relationships	Sharing Faith

Look for Group's Core Belief Bible Study Series books in these other Core Christian Beliefs!

about

Bible Study Series
for senior high

Think for a moment about your young people. When your students walk out of your youth program after they graduate from junior high or high school, what do you want them to know? What foundation do you want them to have so they can make wise choices?

You probably want them to know the essentials of the Christian faith. You want them to base everything they do on the foundational truths of Christianity. Are you meeting this goal?

If you have any doubt that your kids will walk into adulthood knowing and living by the tenets of the Christian faith, then you've picked up the right book. All the books in Group's Core Belief Bible Study Series encourage young people to discover the essentials of Christianity and to put those essentials into practice. Let us explain...

What Is Group's Core Belief Bible Study Series?

Group's Core Belief Bible Study Series is a biblically in-depth study series for junior high and senior high teenagers. This Bible study series utilizes four defining commitments to create each study. These "plumb lines" provide structure and continuity for every activity, study, project, and discussion. They are:

● **A Commitment to Biblical Depth**—Core Belief Bible Study Series is founded on the belief that kids not only *can* understand the deeper truths of the Bible but also *want* to understand them. Therefore, the activities and studies in this series strive to explain the "why" behind every truth we explore. That way, kids learn principles, not just rules.

● **A Commitment to Relevance**—Most kids aren't interested in abstract theories or doctrines about the universe. They want to know how to live successfully right now, today, in the heat of problems they can't ignore. Because of this, each study connects a real-life need with biblical principles that speak directly to that need. This study series finally bridges the gap between Bible truths and the real-world issues kids face.

● **A Commitment to Variety**—Today's young people have been raised in a sound bite world. They demand variety. For that reason, no two meetings in this study series are shaped exactly the same.

● **A Commitment to Active and Interactive Learning**—Active learning is learning by doing. Interactive learning simply takes active learning a step further by having kids teach each other what they've learned. It's a process that helps kids internalize and remember their discoveries.

For a more detailed description of these concepts, see the section titled "Why Active and Interactive Learning Works With Teenagers" beginning on page 55.

So how can you accomplish all this in a set of four easy-to-lead Bible studies? By weaving together various "power" elements to produce a fun experience that leaves kids challenged and encouraged.

Turn the page to take a look at some of the power elements used in this series.

- **A Relevant Topic**—More than ever before, kids live in the now. What matters to them and what attracts their hearts is what's happening in their world at this moment. For this reason, every Core Belief Bible Study focuses on a particular hot topic that kids care about.

- **A Core Christian Belief**—Group's Core Belief Bible Study Series organizes the wealth of Christian truth and experience into twenty-four Core Christian Belief categories. These twenty-four headings act as umbrellas for a collection of detailed beliefs that define Christianity and set it apart from the world and every other religion. Each book in this series features one Core Christian Belief with lessons suited for junior high or senior high students.

  "But," you ask, "won't my kids be bored talking about all these spiritual beliefs?" No way! As a youth leader, you know the value of using hot topics to connect with young people. Ultimately teenagers talk about issues because they're searching for meaning in their lives. They want to find the one equation that will make sense of all the confusing events happening around them. Each Core Belief Bible Study answers that need by connecting a hot topic with a powerful Christian principle. Kids walk away from the study with something more solid than just the shifting ebb and flow of their own opinions. They walk away with a deeper understanding of their Christian faith.

- **The Point**—This simple statement is designed to be the intersection between the Core Christian Belief and the hot topic. Everything in the study ultimately focuses on The Point so that kids study it and allow it time to sink into their hearts.

- **The Study at a Glance**—A quick look at this chart will tell you what kids will do, how long it will take them to do it, and what supplies you'll need to get it done.

Helpful Stuff 11

• **The Bible Connection**—This is the power base of each study. Whether it's just one verse or several chapters, The Bible Connection provides the vital link between kids' minds and their hearts. The content of each Core Belief Bible Study reflects the belief that the true power of God—the power to expose, heal, and change kids' lives—is contained in his Word.

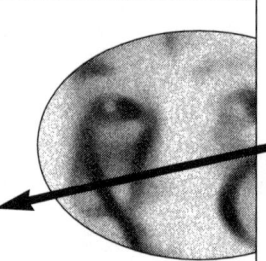

THE POINT OF *BETRAYED!*:

God is love.

THE BIBLE CONNECTION
1 JOHN 4:7-21   The Apostle John explains the nature and definition of perfect love.

In this study, kids will compare the imperfect love defined in real-life stories of betrayal to God's definition of perfect love.

By making this comparison, kids can discover that God is love and therefore incapable of betraying them. Then they'll be able to recognize the incredible opportunity God offers to experience the only relationship worthy of their absolute trust.

Explore the verses in The Bible Connect mation in the Depthfinder boxes througho understanding of how these Scriptures con

THE STUDY

DISCUSSION STARTER ▼

Jump-Start (up to 5 minutes) As kids arrive, ask them to th common themes in movies, books, TV sho have kids each contribute ideas for a ma two other kids in the room and sharing sider providing copies of People maga what's currently showing on televisi their suggestions, write their responses on **come up with a lot of great id ent, look through this list an try to disc ments most of these theme have in com**

After kids make several s gestions, ment responses are connected with the idea of bet

• **Why do you think etrayal is such a**

LEADER TIP for The Study

Because this topic can be so powerful and relevant to kids' lives, your group members may be tempted to get caught up in issues and lose sight of the deeper biblical principle found in The Point. Help your kids grasp The Point by guiding kids to focus on the biblical investigation and discussing how God's truth connects with reality in their lives.

DEPTHFINDER   UNDERSTANDING INTEGRITY

Your students may not be entirely familiar with the meaning of integrity, especially as it might apply to God's character in the Trinity. Use these definitions (taken from Webster's II New Riverside Dictionary) and other information to help you guide kids toward a better understanding of how God maintains integrity through the three expressions of the Trinity.

Integrity: 1. Firm adherence to a code or standard of values. 2. The state of being unimpaired. 3. The quality or condition of being undivided.

Synonyms for integrity include probity, completeness, wholeness, soundness, and perfection.

Our word "integrity" comes from the Latin word *integritas*, which means soundness. *Integritas* is also the root of the word "integer," which means "whole or complete," as in a "whole" number.

The Hebrew word that's often translated "integrity" (for example, in Psalm 25:21 [NIV]) is *tam*. It means whole, perfect, sincere, and honest.

CREATIVE GOD-EXPLORATION ▼

Top Hats (18 to 20 minutes) Form three groups, with each trio member from the previous activity going to a different group. Give each group Bibles, paper, and pens, and assign each group a different hat God wears: Father, Son, or Holy Spirit.

• **Depthfinder Boxes**—These informative sidelights located throughout each study add insight into a particular passage, word, historical fact, or Christian doctrine. Depthfinder boxes also provide insight into teen culture, adolescent development, current events, and philosophy.

holy Profiles

Your assigned Bible passage describes how a particular person or group responded when confronted with God's holiness. Use the information in your passage to help your group discuss the questions below. Then use your flashlights to teach the other two groups what you discover.

■ Based on your passage, what does holiness look like?

■ What does holiness sound like?

■ When people see God's holiness, how does it affect them?

■ How is this response to God's holiness like humility?

■ Based on your passage, how would you describe humility?

■ Why is humility an appropriate human response to God's holiness?

■ Based on what you see in your passage, do you think you are a humble person? Why or why not?

■ What's one way you could develop humility in your life this week?

Permission to photocopy this handout from Group's Core Belief Bible Study Series granted for local church use.
Copyright © Group Publishing, Inc., Box 481, Loveland, CO 80539.

• **Leader Tips**—These handy information boxes coach you through the study, offering helpful suggestions on everything from altering activities for different-sized groups to streamlining discussions to using effective discipline techniques.

• **Handouts**—Most Core Belief Bible Studies include photocopiable handouts to use with your group. Handouts might take the form of a fun game, a lively discussion starter, or a challenging study page for kids to take home—anything to make your study more meaningful and effective.

Helpful Stuff   12

The Last Word on Core Belief Bible Studies

Soon after you begin to use Group's Core Belief Bible Study Series, you'll see signs of real growth in your group members. Your kids will gain a deeper understanding of the Bible and of their own Christian faith. They'll see more clearly how a relationship with Jesus affects their daily lives. And they'll grow closer to God.

But that's not all. You'll also see kids grow closer to one another.

That's because this series is founded on the principle that Christian faith grows best in the context of relationship. Each study uses a variety of interactive pairs and small groups and always includes discussion questions that promote deeper relationships. The friendships kids will build through this study series will enable them to grow *together* toward a deeper relationship with God.

Grave Concerns

THE ISSUE: Death

WHY TEENAGERS ARE TERRIFIED OF DYING

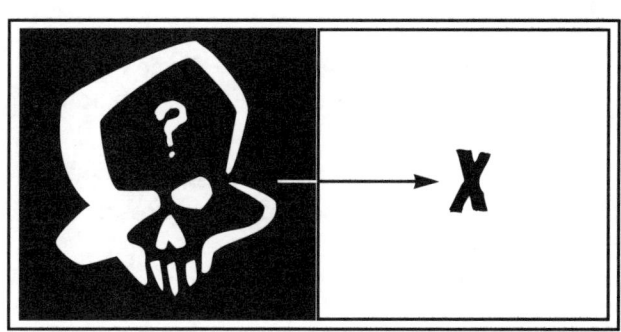

by James Selman

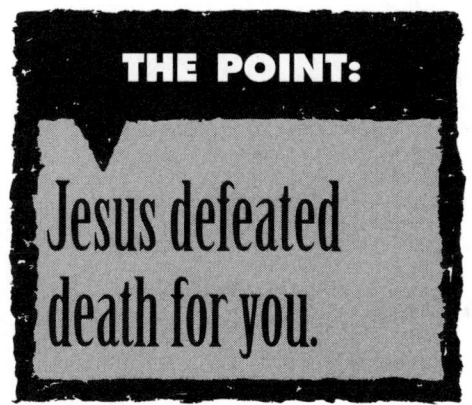

THE POINT:
Jesus defeated death for you.

■ Death is a mystery. For some people, death ranks as their greatest fear. For others, death is their greatest joy. For some it brings a sweet relief from pain. For others, it is the ultimate sorrow. ■ Death can be frightening. Yet your kids face it every day. They see it on the news, on the streets, and in the faces of friends who've lost the hope to live. ■ We may want to protect kids from facing death, but we can't. Yet we can help them face it with courage and faith. ■ This study guides your students in exploring what God says about death and unveils the truth that lies at the heart of our Christian faith—that Jesus defeated death for us on the cross.

The Study AT A GLANCE

SECTION	MINUTES	WHAT STUDENTS WILL DO	SUPPLIES
Relational Time	5 to 10	ROOM OF DEATH—Decorate the room to look like a cemetery.	Black markers, newsprint, tape, scissors
Investigation of Death	up to 5	SEPARATION—Come up with things that describe death as separation.	Newsprint, marker, paper, pens, black licorice sticks
	10 to 15	GOOD FROM BAD?— Act out things that appear bad but are sometimes good.	Bible
Investigation of Life	20 to 25	DEATH TO LIFE—Transform the meeting room from "death" to "life" based on truths in Scripture.	Newsprint, tape, colored markers, scissors, "Really Knowing God's Love" handouts (pp. 22-23), pens
Creative Worship	5 to 10	THE GREATEST LOVE—Form a cross and listen to lyrics about God's love.	Masking tape, cassette or CD of "There Is a Greater Love" by Wayne Watson (or something similar), cassette or CD player

notes:

THE POINT OF *GRAVE CONCERNS:*

Jesus defeated death for you.

THE BIBLE CONNECTION

JOHN 1:12; EPHESIANS 2:4-5a, 8-9; 1 JOHN 5:11-13	These passages describe how we can have God's gift of eternal life.
HEBREWS 2:14-18	The author talks about Jesus' becoming a man to understand our fears and take them away.

I n this study, kids will create an atmosphere of death and join in activities that demonstrate how death is separation from life. Then they'll compare Scripture passages that describe how <u>Jesus defeated death for us.</u>

Through these experiences kids will discover that Jesus' love led him to suffer and die so that they wouldn't be separated from him for eternity.

Explore the verses in The Bible Connection, then examine the information in the Depthfinder boxes throughout the study to gain a deeper understanding of how these Scriptures connect with your young people.

LEADER TIP for The Study

Whenever you tell groups to discuss a list of questions, write the questions on newsprint and tape the newsprint to the wall. That way all groups can discuss the questions at their own pace.

THE STUDY

RELATIONAL TIME ▼

Room of Death (5 to 10 minutes) As the kids enter, set out newsprint, tape, scissors, and black markers. Tell kids to transform the room to look like a cemetery or anything that has to do with death. For example, kids might draw coffins or tombstones or create paper skeletons to make the atmosphere gloomy. Also, dim the lights by covering the lighting fixtures or turning off some of the lights.

Once kids are finished, gather everyone together and ask:
● **What scares you most about death?**
● **If you could choose how you'd like to die, what would you choose?**

LEADER TIP for Room of Death

You may even want to supply makeup so kids and adult leaders can make themselves look dead.

Grave Concerns 17

LEADER TIP for Room of Death

Teenagers like to tell and hear stories. While you're transforming the room, have kids tell stories of their experiences with death. Use this opportunity to listen to them. Ask kids questions about their experiences. And don't hesitate to share your own stories about death. This kind of listening and personal sharing can be one of the most valuable things you can do to build trust with your kids.

DEPTHFINDER — UNDERSTANDING THE BIBLE

The Greek word for death (thanatos) means the separation of the soul from the body. In the New Testament, however, the word always refers to the separation from God we experience because of sin.

Thankfully, according to Ephesians 2:1-10, the barrier that separates us from God was destroyed through Jesus. That's the great news of Jesus' resurrection—that <u>Jesus defeated death for us</u> so we could have eternal life with him.

● **What would be the worst kind of death you could think of?**

Say: **We're going to talk a lot about death today, but my hope is that it won't be depressing for us. That's because I want you to discover a powerful truth about our Christian faith: that <u>Jesus defeated death for all of us,</u> so we don't have to fear death anymore.**

INVESTIGATION OF DEATH ▼

Separation (up to 5 minutes)

Say: **Now that we've got the right atmosphere, let's get started.** Ask:

● **How would you define death?**

Write kids' definitions on newsprint, then say: **All of these definitions reflect some powerful ideas about death. But for our study today, we'll define death as separation. Basically, death means to separate one thing from another. For example, physical death is separation from physical life.**

Form groups of four, and distribute pens and paper. Tell groups they have two minutes to each create a list of unique examples that illustrate death as the separation of one thing from another. Some examples might be the death of a friendship (the separation of friends) or the death of a marriage (the separation of two people that God has joined together).

After two minutes, ask one of the groups to give all its answers, and have the other groups check their lists for those same responses (write all of the kids' responses on newsprint for later reference). If more than one group has the same response, have them all draw an X over that answer. Continue this process until all the groups have given their examples. Then see which group has the most unique responses, and reward each member of that group with a stick of black licorice. Ask:

● **What does it feel like to be separated from something or someone important to you?**

● **What kinds of fears do these "deaths" cause?**

Say: **All of the fears we feel in life—fear of meeting new people, fear of being alone, fear of being abandoned, fear of failure—can be traced back to one root fear—the fear of death. That's why <u>Jesus defeated death for you.</u> By**

Grave Concerns 18

overcoming death, he's provided a way for you to be free of all your fears. Let's explore how Jesus did this and what that means for you today.

Good From Bad? (10 to 15 minutes)

Form trios. Have trios think of one *bad* thing that becomes *good* when used in a different way. Warn them that after they come up with an example, they must devise a creative way to act it out for the rest of the class. For example, trios might act out how explosives can be used to put out an oil or gas fire, how snake venom can be used to make antivenin, or how a weakened or partial virus can be used to vaccinate against disease. When trios are ready, have them each demonstrate their actions to the rest of the group. Have the rest of the kids try to guess each "good from bad" situation.

When everyone is finished, have students tell each person in their trio about a time when they've seen that person handle a bad situation in a good way.

When trios finish, call everyone together and have a volunteer read aloud Hebrews 2:14-18. Say: **Jesus used something that was bad—death—to defeat the power of death and the fear that goes with it. Jesus was ridiculed, beaten, and killed so we could have the chance to be saved from being eternally separated from God. <u>Jesus defeated death for you.</u> So, as Christians, even though we still die physically, we don't have to be afraid of death anymore. Physical death is simply a doorway to everlasting life.**

> **LEADER TIP for The Study**
>
> Because this topic can be so powerful and relevant to kids' lives, your group members may be tempted to get caught up in issues and lose sight of the deeper biblical principle found in The Point. Help your kids grasp The Point by guiding them to focus on the biblical investigation and discussing how God's truth connects with reality in their lives.

DEPTH FINDER — THE FEAR OF DYING

The fear of dying is universal. It's part of the nature of humanity. As young people, your students may fear death because of how it can affect them. Younger teenagers often fear death because it takes away their parents and leaves them with no one to care for them. Older kids may think of death as an enemy because it can take away the blossoming life that they're just beginning to experience.

Whatever their fears, kids today are expressing deeper concerns about death than ever before. The main question on their minds—and the question they may ask you—is, "Why? Why do we have to die?"

The answer is sin. God's moral law demands death as the payment for sin—any sin. That truth may not be comforting for kids, but it can help them understand that death entered the world because humanity rejected God, not because he rejected humanity.

Fortunately for Christians, death has no real power. Jesus made a spectacle of death on the cross (see Colossians 2:15). And although death still holds sway over life in the physical realm, it has absolutely no eternal power, and even the power it has now will someday be taken away (see 1 Corinthians 15:26, 52-53). God has saved Christians from the eternal consequences of death, so we don't have to fear it anymore.

INVESTIGATION OF LIFE ▼

Death to Life (20 to 25 minutes)

Open this activity by praying: **God, thank you for the love that you've given to us even though we don't deserve it. Thank you for giving us your Son, Jesus, who defeated death for us so that we don't have to fear death. Help us now to understand more about your love for us. Amen.**

Have kids form three groups. Give each student a photocopy of the "Really Knowing God's Love" handout (pp. 22-23) and a pen. Assign a different passage to each group, then say: **Read your assigned passage, and answer the questions listed below it. Be prepared to read your passage and report your answers to the rest of the class.**

After five minutes, say: **God doesn't want to be separated from us. He loves us so much that he made a way for us to always be near him, even after we're separated from physical life.**

Have Group 1 report its findings to the rest of the class. After it finishes, ask the whole group:

● **Do you ever have doubts about your faith?**

● **Do you ever think that because you doubt, or feel afraid of death, or have questions, that God isn't happy with you? Why or why not?**

Say: **Just because we have fear or questions about death doesn't mean that God will disown us. He loves us. Let's see how God has shown his love to us.**

Have Groups 2 and 3 report their findings to the whole class. When they're finished, say: **All you have to do to make sure you're not separated from God is to believe in Jesus and trust in what he has done for you. Jesus defeated death for you by offering himself as a sacrifice for your sin.**

Have kids use newsprint, colored markers, scissors, and tape to transform the room from a "Room of Death" to a "Room of Life in Christ." Ask kids to place pictures, symbols, or words around the room that describe how Jesus overcomes death in our lives and what he provides for Christians after they die. Encourage kids to refer to the Bible passages on their handouts for inspiration.

CREATIVE WORSHIP ▼

The Greatest Love (5 to 10 minutes)

When kids finish transforming the room, have them use masking tape to create an outline of a large cross on the floor. Ask students to kneel on or near the cross.

Say: **We can have a new life because of God's love. Let's close today by listening to a song about God's special love for us. As you listen, pray silently and thank God for sending Jesus to defeat death for us.**

Play the song "There Is a Greater Love" from *How Time Flies* by Wayne Watson. If you don't have a copy of the song, you can substitute any song that describes God's love for us. Or simply read aloud the words of an appropriate hymn, such as "Because He Lives" or "When I Survey the Wondrous Cross."

When the song is over, close by saying: **God doesn't promise that all your feelings of fear or all your troubles will go away. But he does promise that he'll go through them all with you and give you the strength you need to overcome your fears.**

LEADER TIP for The Greatest Love

If you'd like to purchase a copy of the song "There Is a Greater Love" by Wayne Watson, you can contact Word, Inc., at (817) 772-4200. Ask for the CD or cassette titled *How Time Flies*.

DEPTHFINDER — UNDERSTANDING THE BIBLE

The word "help" in Hebrews 2:16 and 18 means to "catch" or "take hold of." The picture the word describes is that of a father on a family picnic. The father's small child has scaled a tree and is terrified to come down. The father runs under the child and says, "Jump, and Daddy will catch you." That's the image this word evokes.

Jesus knew our desperate situation and loved us so much that he willingly ran to help us. If we'll trust him, he'll save us from the consequences of our sin.

Really Knowing God's Love

Really   Knowing

Group 1

Read this passage:

"This is what God told us: God has given us eternal life, and this life is in his Son. Whoever has the Son has life, but whoever does not have the Son of God does not have life. I write this letter to you who believe in the Son of God so you will know you have eternal life" (1 John 5:11-13).

Discuss these questions:

- Where can we find eternal life?
- Some say there are "many paths" to God. According to this passage, can you have eternal life without Jesus Christ? Why or why not?

Permission to photocopy this handout from Group's Core Belief Bible Study Series granted for local church use. Copyright © Group Publishing, Inc., P.O. Box 481, Loveland, CO 80539.

God's Love

Group 2

Read this passage:

"But God's mercy is great, and he loved us very much. Though we were spiritually dead because of the things we did against God, he gave us new life with Christ...I mean that you have been saved by grace through believing. You did not save yourselves; it was a gift from God. It was not the result of your own efforts, so you cannot brag about it" (Ephesians 2:4-5a, 8-9).

Discuss these questions:
- Why did God offer Jesus as a gift to bring us new life?
- According to the passage, is there anything you can do to earn eternal life with God? Explain.
- What is it that keeps you from being separated from God eternally?

Group 3

Read this passage:

"But to all who did accept him and believe in him he gave the right to become children of God" (John 1:12).

Discuss these questions:
- Who can become a child of God?
- What do you have to do to become a child of God?

THE ISSUE: Cults

OPENING KIDS' EYES TO THE LURE OF CULTS

by Bob Buller

THE POINT:

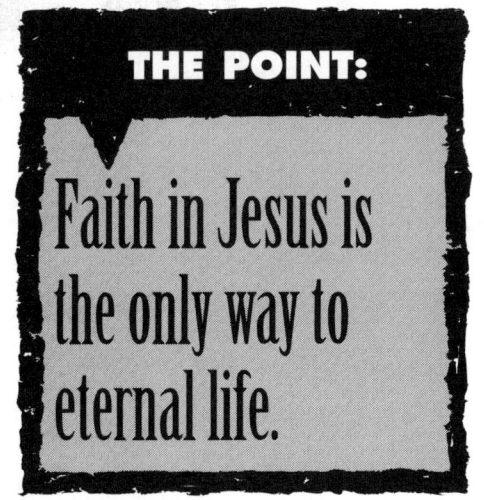

Faith in Jesus is the only way to eternal life.

■ Your students know that the world is a dangerous place. They're painfully aware of guns in schools, drugs on the corner, sexually transmitted diseases, physical abuse in the home, and a thousand other threats to their safety and happiness. ■ However, for all their street smarts, most kids are oblivious to one threat that's just as dangerous as a gun to the head or a needle in the arm: cults. ■ These days most cult members don't shave their heads, wear strange robes, or stand on street corners chanting mantras. In most cases, today's cult member looks, thinks, and acts just like you. ■ And your kids. ■ This study unmasks cults and cult leaders so kids can recognize counterfeit beliefs about salvation and the church and embrace the truth that faith in Jesus is the only way to eternal life.

The Study
AT A GLANCE

SECTION	MINUTES	WHAT STUDENTS WILL DO	SUPPLIES
Group Transformation	10 to 15	CULT CLASSICS—Transform themselves to demonstrate what they think cult members look like.	Paper, pencils, various clothing items
Bible Exploration	10 to 15	YOU CAN'T TRUST EVERYONE—Study Matthew 7:15-23 to learn how cult leaders are like false prophets.	Bibles, index cards, pencils
	15 to 20	LOOKS MAY BE DECEIVING—Based on new information, transform themselves to demonstrate what cults really look like.	"Cult Clues" handouts (pp. 32-33)
Creative Comparison	5 to 10	NO CONTEST!—Learn from John 14:6-7 and 1 Timothy 2:5-6 how Jesus is superior to any cult leader.	Bibles, index cards, pencils, masking tape, marker
Action Plan	up to 5	HELPING A FRIEND—Brainstorm ways to help friends who are influenced by cults.	Newsprint, tape, markers

notes:

THE POINT OF *CULT REPELLENT:*

Faith in Jesus is the only way to eternal life.

THE BIBLE CONNECTION

MATTHEW 7:15-23	Jesus warns against the dangers of following false prophets.
JOHN 14:6-7	Jesus states that he is the only way to the Father.
1 TIMOTHY 2:5-6	Paul teaches that Jesus is the only mediator between God and humans.

In this study, kids will act out cult behavior to discover how they can recognize a cult when they see one. They'll also talk about how today's cult leaders are like the false prophets Jesus warned us about.

Through these experiences, kids will learn how to avoid being lured into cults. They'll also discover why Jesus is the only person they can fully trust to give them the gift of eternal life.

Explore the verses in The Bible Connection, then examine the information in the Depthfinder boxes throughout the study to gain a deeper understanding of how these Scriptures connect with your young people.

LEADER TIP for The Study
Whenever groups discuss a list of questions, write the questions on newsprint and tape the newsprint to the wall so groups can answer the questions at their own pace.

THE STUDY

GROUP TRANSFORMATION ▼

Cult Classics (10 to 15 minutes) Form three groups, and have each group select a Recorder. Give each Recorder a sheet of paper and a pencil. Instruct group members to brainstorm words and phrases that define what a cult is or that describe what a cult does. Tell Recorders to write down everyone's ideas.

Cult Repellent   27

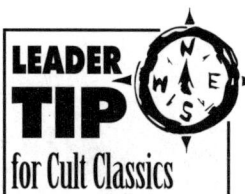

Leader TIP for Cult Classics

If you have more than thirty students, you might consider forming six groups instead of three, then adjusting the activities throughout the study accordingly. Forming more groups will allow kids to participate more fully in the discussions and activities.

After a few minutes, set out various articles of clothing or materials such as towels or bedsheets that kids can use to create costumes. Then say: **Based on the information you've come up with, I want you to transform your entire group into a cult. Choose a cult "leader" from among your group members, and decide what characteristics or practices will make your group an official cult. You can use any of the supplies I've provided or anything else in the room to help you transform yourselves. Go!**

Give groups several minutes to transform, then have groups take turns presenting themselves to the rest of the class. Have students guess what makes each group a true cult.

After groups present their transformations, form trios that include one person from each of the three groups. Have trios discuss the following questions:

● **How were our presentations of cults similar? different?**
● **How hard is it to recognize a cult when you encounter one?**
● **How would you respond if you were asked to join a cult? Why?**

Say: **Since <u>faith in Jesus is the only way to eternal life,</u> we should avoid cults that claim there are other ways to know God. However, that's not always as easy as it sounds. Jesus taught that some cults and cult leaders are much harder to spot than the ones you've just portrayed. So today we're going to learn how to recognize a cult when we see one.**

BIBLE EXPLORATION ▼

You Can't Trust Everyone (10 to 15 minutes) Have kids reform the three original groups. Give everyone an index card and a pencil. Assign one of the following questions to each group:

● **How are false prophets like true prophets? different?**
● **What kinds of bad "fruit" will we see in false prophets?**
● **What may be the consequences of trusting a false prophet?**

Instruct the groups to read Matthew 7:15-23 and discuss how the biblical passage answers their assigned questions. Have kids jot down ideas from their discussions. They'll report what they learn to members of the other groups.

After two minutes, have kids reform the trios from the "Cult Classics" discussion. Tell kids to each take thirty seconds to explain how the Bible passage answers their assigned question. After everyone has reported, have trios discuss the following questions:

● **How are cult leaders like false prophets? different?**
● **How might cult leaders seem similar to true Christian leaders? different?**
● **How can we recognize a cult leader when we see one?**
● **What might be the consequences of following a cult leader?**

Say: **The cult leaders of today, like the false prophets of Jesus' day, are sometimes difficult to spot. Cult leaders often look and**

Cult Repellent 28

> ## DEPTHFINDER   UNDERSTANDING THE BIBLE
>
> In Matthew 7:15-23, Jesus uses two metaphors to teach his listeners how to recognize false prophets.
>
> First, false prophets are like wolves dressed in sheepskins. They may look like one of the flock from a distance, but closer scrutiny and time always reveal the wolves' true identities. It's their nature to act like wolves, and eventually they'll try to consume the sheep.
>
> Second, false prophets are like thorn bushes and thistles that can't produce edible fruit. Although the berries on the buckthorn may resemble grapes and the flowers on certain thistles may look like blooming figs, closer inspection reveals that these plants bear only "bad fruit."
>
> Jesus' point is that we must carefully and patiently examine leaders to discern their true nature and the "fruit" that their nature produces.

act like Christians, but they secretly distort the foundational Christian belief that <u>faith in Jesus is the only way to eternal life.</u> That's why we need to know how to see through a cult leader's positive image to the negative reality that lurks under the surface.

Looks May Be Deceiving (15 to 20 minutes)

Have kids return to their three original groups. Give each person a photocopy of the "Cult Clues" handout (pp. 32-33). Read aloud the summary at the beginning of the handout, then assign each group one section of the handout. Say: **Your last cult transformation was based on your own impressions of what cults are like. Now I want you to transform your group into a new cult. This time, base your group's transformation on the information provided in your assigned section of the handout.**

Give groups several minutes to prepare, then have groups take turns presenting themselves to the rest of the class. As groups make their presentations, ask them to explain how their cult reflects the information in the handout.

Once the presentations are finished, have kids return to their trios to discuss these questions:

● **How were these transformations like the earlier ones? different?**
● **Based on what you've learned, how would you define "cult"?**
● **How do cults appear to be Christian? How are cults different from true Christianity?**
● **Which cult characteristics would be attractive to your friends?**
● **What bad "fruit" can you look for in organizations to learn whether they might be cultic?**

Have kids identify one good "fruit" they see in the life of each member of their trio that will help him or her avoid being lured into a cult. For example, someone might say, "Courtney, your knowledge of God's Word will help you spot false teachings."

LEADER TIP for Looks May Be Deceiving

Most of your kids will act out the second transformation in their normal clothes. However, if one or more of the groups creates costumes for the second transformation, have the three groups each discuss whether they'll really be able to recognize cult members by the way they dress or behave in public.

DEPTHFINDER: WHAT MAKES A CULT?

Christians often identify cults on the basis of their deviation from the theological truths taught in the Bible. Unfortunately, this approach to cult identification fails as often as it succeeds. Many cults claim to have the correct interpretation of the Bible, so the battle for truth is reduced to endless bickering over interpretations. Also, most "theological" definitions of "cult" neglect the fact that cults often inflict significant psychological and social damage on their members. Therefore, instead of focusing on a theological definition, this study examines typical cult behavior. This approach teaches kids to identify cults by their actions as well as their beliefs.

In terms of theology, many cults appear to be genuinely Christian. However, cults inevitably distort, deny, or add to some part of Christian truth. Also, cults often employ various methods of manipulation to destroy members' self-identity and to control thoughts and actions. Even as cults promise to meet members' social needs through nurturing relationships and a caring environment, they also pressure members to isolate themselves from family members, friends, and society.

Describing cults in these terms can help your kids recognize the different ways any group can be cultic. Some groups may be socially nurturing but theologically incorrect; others may be theologically sound but psychologically damaging. In either case, kids need to beware of the cultic tendencies of all the groups they encounter.

After everyone has shared, say: **Cult leaders often set themselves up as equal—or even superior—to Jesus. But cult leaders are never able to offer us true salvation. Ultimately, they always fail to deliver what they promise. That's because <u>faith in Jesus is the only way to eternal life.</u>**

CREATIVE COMPARISON ▼

LEADER TIP for No Contest!
If someone identifies a positive quality of Jesus that doesn't correspond to any of the negative characteristics, simply write the quality on an index card and tape it to "Jesus."

No Contest! (5 to 10 minutes) Ask for a volunteer "cult leader," and have that person stand where everyone can see him or her. Have kids call out any negative characteristics of cult leaders they've discovered during the study. For example, someone might say, "Cult leaders tell lies" or "Cult leaders take advantage of people." Write each characteristic on an index card, and tape it to the cult leader. After kids call out five or six characteristics, instruct half the class to read John 14:6-7 and the other half to read 1 Timothy 2:5-6.

After the kids read their passages, ask for a volunteer "Jesus" to stand beside the cult leader. Have kids call out positive qualities of Jesus—based on the Scripture passages—that cancel out the cult leader's negative characteristics. For example, someone might say, "Jesus is the truth" or "Jesus works for our benefit." Each time someone calls out a positive quality, remove the index card with the corresponding negative characteristic from the cult leader, cross out the negative characteristic with a marker, write the positive quality on an index card, and tape it

Cult Repellent 30

to "Jesus." Have kids call out positive qualities of Jesus until every negative characteristic of the cult leader has been canceled out.

Say: **Cults and cult leaders often claim that they hold the key to a deeper relationship with God. But once you compare cult leaders with Jesus, the truth becomes clear: Faith in Jesus is the only way to eternal life.**

Thank the volunteers, and have "Jesus" remove the index cards from his or her clothing.

ACTION PLAN ▼

Helping a Friend (up to 5 minutes)

Ask the entire group to brainstorm ways they might help a friend who's been lured into a cult. Tape up a sheet of newsprint, and record everyone's ideas on it.

Then distribute markers, and have each person write a short prayer on the newsprint for their specific needs. For example, some students might want God to show them how to help their friends, while others might want God to help them recognize and resist the lure of cults.

After everyone is finished writing a prayer, close the meeting with a spoken prayer, asking God to protect kids from the deception of cults and thanking him for sending Jesus, the only true source of eternal life.

> **LEADER TIP for The Study**
>
> Because this topic can be so powerful and relevant to kids' lives, your group members may be tempted to get caught up in issues and lose sight of the deeper biblical principle found in The Point. Help your kids grasp The Point by guiding them to focus on the biblical investigation and discussing how God's truth connects with reality in their lives.

DEPTHFINDER: HOW TO HELP SOMEONE WHO'S IN A CULT

Getting someone out of a cult can be a long, difficult process that requires great patience and love. Strategies for "intervention" abound, but the most effective approaches always include these ground rules:

- Don't panic or become angry at the person you're trying to help.
- Educate yourself about the specific beliefs and practices of the cult.
- Enlist the aid of former members of the cult, church leaders, and counselors with experience in cult intervention.
- Offer unconditional love and acceptance to the person you're trying to win back.
- Rely upon God for strength, guidance, and the success of your spiritual battle.

For additional information on cults or helping someone who's in a cult, see *Cult-Proofing Your Kids* by Paul R. Martin, *The Lure of the Cults and New Religions* by Ronald M. Enroth, or *Combatting Cult Mind Control* by Steve Hassan.

Cult Clues

Cult members don't always wear strange outfits, distribute literature in airports, or stand on street corners and chant. In fact, most cults are a confused and confusing mix of truth and error, good and bad. Cults are often appealing precisely because they appear to be genuine expressions of true Christianity, but they're ultimately based on damaging lies. The following clues will help you recognize a cult when you see one.

Theological traits

Cults:

- may accept, teach, and promote some Christian beliefs;
- often distort or deny Christian beliefs about Christ;
- emphasize spiritual commitment and service;
- substitute study of cult literature for Bible study;
- appeal to teenagers seeking a deeper relationship with God; and
- claim to be the only ones who understand the truth.

Psychological traits

Cults:

- manipulate people through guilt and fear of judgment;
- provide simple answers to life's complex questions;
- control every area of members' thoughts and lives;
- don't allow members to question the leader's authority;
- offer structure, stability, and security to members; and
- discourage individual freedom and self-expression.

Social traits

Cults:

- pressure members to break ties with friends and family;
- offer love, support, and friendship to people in crises;
- enforce strict rules about eating, sleeping, and free time;
- may organize into a church or "Christian" ministry;
- require members to support and obey a spiritual leader; and
- threaten to expel members who don't follow cult standards.

THE ISSUE: Grace

Running on Empty

HOW JESUS CAN FILL OUR LIVES TO OVERFLOWING

by Lisa Baba Lauffer

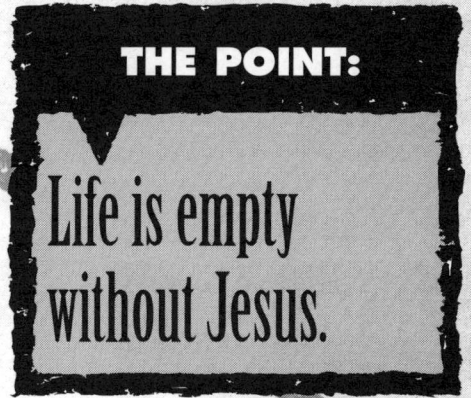

THE POINT:

Life is empty without Jesus.

■ When you think of your senior highers, "empty" is probably not a word that you'd use to describe them. Today's young people seem to lead full lives with school, family, friends, sports, and zillions of other activities. Pay attention to the context in which your students live and move—walls plastered with posters, clothes and books scattered on the floors, radios blaring, ears connected to the telephone, and images flashing on televisions and computer monitors. Today's young people are constantly bombarded with sights and sounds that fill their senses. ■ But if you take the time to look deeper and listen carefully, you'll discover a disturbing trend. Far beneath all the superficial fullness exists a void, an emptiness, a yearning. And no matter what kids—or adults, for that matter—do to drown it out, it still underlies all they say and do. Emptiness is what compels them, and it's relentless. ■ We all try to fill this void in whatever ways we think we can. Some can't listen to its pleas anymore, so they'll do anything to drown out its cries—preoccupy themselves with countless superficial relationships, busy themselves with nonstop activity, or pursue the perfect body through stringent diet and exercise. Others try to fill the void with accomplishments, food, even drugs and alcohol, thinking that if they stuff themselves with these things, maybe the yearning will finally go away. ■ But it doesn't. Because only one "thing" can fill it—Jesus. And until we accept his gift of grace, we'll keep feeling the emptiness inside. This study will bring this truth to light, helping your students understand their need to embark upon and nurture a lifesaving, life-fulfilling relationship with Jesus Christ.

The Study
AT A GLANCE

SECTION	MINUTES	WHAT STUDENTS WILL DO	SUPPLIES
Image Creation	20 to 25	**FULL OR EMPTY?**—Write and tell stories of people, real or imagined, who lead completely fulfilled lives, then readjust their stories to take changing circumstances into account.	Bibles, slips of paper, markers, tape, paper, pencils
Object Lesson 1	10 to 15	**THE BOTTOMLESS BALLOON**—Attempt to keep balloons inflated as they write on the balloons things they think can fulfill their lives.	Bibles, balloons, straight pin, markers
Object Lesson 2	20 to 25	**DRIPPLEY'S BELIEVE IT OR NOT**—Do a science experiment in which cheesecloth holds water in a jar, then compare the logistics of the experiment to the way Jesus fills our lives.	Bibles, cheesecloth, scissors, rubber bands, bottles and jars with small openings, paper cups, water, tape, whole balloons from "The Bottomless Balloon" activity, markers, paper

notes:

THE POINT OF *RUNNING ON EMPTY:*

Life is empty without Jesus.

THE BIBLE CONNECTION

JOHN 1:14, 16-17	John explains that we receive the fullness of grace and truth through Jesus Christ.
ROMANS 8:10-13	Paul explains that we have life if God's Spirit is living in us.
EPHESIANS 2:4-9	Paul explains how God's grace saves us from spiritual deadness.
PHILIPPIANS 3:3-11	Paul describes the emptiness and worthlessness of trusting in anything or anyone except Jesus Christ.

In this study, kids will write stories about completely fulfilled people and then rewrite those stories as circumstances change. They'll also complete object lessons that will illustrate their own inability to achieve true fulfillment in their lives and how Jesus can completely fulfill their lives in ways they'd never expect. Along with these activities, they'll explore Scriptures about the fulfilling nature of grace.

By applying the results of these experiences to their own lives, kids can discover that they can find true fulfillment only when they entrust their lives to Jesus Christ, their Savior.

Explore the verses in The Bible Connection, then examine the information in the Depthfinder boxes throughout the study to gain a deeper understanding of how these Scriptures connect with your young people.

LEADER TIP for The Study

Whenever groups discuss a list of questions, write the questions on newsprint and tape the newsprint to the wall so groups can discuss the questions at their own pace.

BEFORE THE STUDY

For "The Bottomless Balloon" activity, gather a balloon for each student. Using a straight pin, poke ten holes in each balloon. (To do this quickly, take an uninflated balloon, press it flat, then poke through both layers of latex five times.) You'll also need balloons, at least one per student, that do not have holes poked in them. Make sure you keep the poked and unpoked balloons in separate piles.

For the "Drippley's Believe It or Not" activity, gather one bottle or jar for every two students. Jars and bottles with small mouths work best, such as baby-food jars or twelve-ounce soft drink bottles. Then cut the cheesecloth into squares big enough to cover the mouth of the largest bottle you've gathered with about one-half inch of extra cheesecloth in each direction. You'll need one square for each student. If you can't find cheesecloth, you can substitute pantyhose (make sure the squares you cut *do not* have runs in them). You'll also need to fill one paper cup with water for every four students.

Running on Empty 37

THE STUDY

Leader TIP for The Study

For added discussion, play dc Talk's "Like It, Love It, Need It" from their *Jesus Freak* album. Have your young people listen to the lyrics and then discuss what the lyrics say about how to gain true fulfillment in life.

IMAGE CREATION ▼

Full or Empty? (20 to 25 minutes) Have students form four groups. Hand each group slips of paper, markers, sheets of paper, pencils, and tape. Say: **Today we're going to talk about how we can lead full lives—particularly the role that God's grace plays in having a full life. With your group, think of a person that has the most full life you could possibly imagine. This person can be real, a combination of people you know, or a completely imaginary person. You can define "full life" however you wish. When you've determined who this person is, write a story about his or her life that includes how the person developed the fullness in his or her life.**

As you create this person, have someone in your group volunteer to portray him or her. Using the slips of paper I've given you, label your person according to the things that make that person's life full. For example, if your person has a lot of money, tape a slip of paper labeled "money" to your volunteer's pocket.

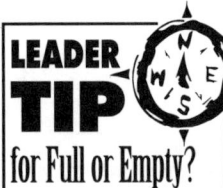

Leader TIP for Full or Empty?

For added entertainment, bring skit props and clothes for groups to use in creating and depicting their people.

Allow groups ten minutes to create their people. Then have each group present its person by reading the story of how that person became so fulfilled and pointing out the labels taped to the volunteer.

After all the presentations, say: **Wow. Your people seem to have it all together. But I wonder whether they'd lead such full lives if even one of their positive circumstances was taken away from them.** Pull one label from each group's volunteer, and say: **Now that some circumstances have changed in your person's life, how does that affect the fullness of your person's life? Revise your story to reflect how the loss affects your person and how he or she copes with his or her loss.**

After three minutes, have groups share what their people lost and read their revised stories to the class. Then have kids form pairs within their groups to discuss these questions:

● **Before the changes took place, why did your person have a full life?**

● **How did the changes affect your person? Did he or she still have a full life? Why or why not?**

● **How much are you like your group's person before the changes? After the changes? Explain.**

● **Read Philippians 3:3-6. According to Paul, what made his life full before he met Christ? Do you think those things really fulfilled him? Why or why not?**

● **How full is your life? Why?**

When pairs have finished their discussions, invite students to share any insights they have. Then say: **We all want to lead full lives, but**

Leader TIP for The Study

Because this topic can be so powerful and relevant to kids' lives, your group members may be tempted to get caught up in issues and lose sight of the deeper biblical principle found in The Point. Help your kids grasp The Point by guiding them to focus on the biblical investigation and discussing how God's truth connects with reality in their lives.

Running on Empty 38

> # DEPTHFINDER
> ## UNDERSTANDING PAUL'S PASSION FOR GRACE
>
> In both Ephesians 2:1-9 and Philippians 3:3-11, the Apostle Paul expresses how God's grace saves us and, ultimately, fulfills our lives. Grace was Paul's favorite theme, and he sprinkled it liberally throughout his epistles. According to author and pastor Frederick Buechner, "At the start of virtually every one of his letters, grace is what Saint Paul wishes his friends first, even before mercy, even before peace, and no matter how much of a hurry he is in to get on with the main business of the letter, he always points out that this grace he wishes them is 'from God our Father and the Lord Jesus Christ' because he wants there to be absolutely no doubt about that. Grace is the best he can wish them because grace is the best he himself ever received."
>
> (Frederick Buechner, *The Longing for Home*)

none of us has a very good handle on how to accomplish that feat. As we saw in our activity, even those who seem to have it all can easily lose their grip on fulfillment. And as we'll discover through today's study, even Paul, an exemplary Jew and Pharisee of his day, didn't find fulfillment in his rank or his works. Instead, he discovered that <u>life is empty without Jesus.</u>

Before we move on, pray with your partner. Ask God to use today's study to show you and your partner how to gain true fulfillment through his Son, Jesus Christ.

OBJECT LESSON 1 ▼

The Bottomless Balloon
(10 to 15 minutes)

When pairs have finished praying, hand each student a balloon with holes poked in it and a marker. Don't say anything to students about the holes poked in the balloons.

Say: **Let's bring this point a little closer to home. Think for a moment of all the things that could make your life so complete that you could want absolutely nothing more. As you do this, inflate your balloon, and write on the balloon each item you think of. Don't tie your balloon off, but make sure to keep your balloon inflated during the whole activity.**

When students have finished writing their lists, have kids return to their pairs from the previous activity. Then have each pair find another pair to form a foursome. Have foursomes discuss these questions:

● **What things did you write on your balloon? Why do you think those things could bring you a full life?**

● **How successful were you at keeping your balloon inflated? What did it take for you to keep your balloon inflated?**

● **How was attempting to keep your balloon inflated like attempting to gain fulfillment through the things you wrote on your balloon? How was it different?**

LEADER TIP
for The Bottomless Balloon

In most cases, your students will create a large list of items that would contribute to a fulfilled life, and this will work well to support the point of the study. However, some of your students may have already found the true source of fulfillment. These students may simply write "Jesus Christ" on their balloons. If this happens, discreetly give these students balloons without holes in them and instruct these students to rewrite their "lists" on their new balloons.

Running on Empty 39

LEADER TIP
for The Bottomless Balloon

Some kids may not be able to write anything on their balloons because their balloons may deflate too quickly or pop. If this happens, include questions in your discussion such as:
- What would you have written on your balloon if you could've kept it inflated?
- Was it frustrating to try and write on your balloon?
- How was trying to write on your balloon like attempting to gain fulfillment through the things you were trying to write?

DEPTH FINDER — UNDERSTANDING GRACE

Grace is such a deceptively simple concept. Accept God's gift of it through Jesus Christ, and you've received salvation for all eternity. And yet for those of us in Western culture with our hallowed work ethic, that one simple action—mere acceptance—never seems to be enough. We're accustomed to "earning our pay," and we apply that mentality to our eternal destiny. After all, why should salvation be any different from the other rewards we earn?

But in his letter to the Ephesians, Paul makes it clear that grace is all we need. In Ephesians 2:8-9, he says, "I mean that you have been saved by grace through believing. You did not save yourselves; it was a gift from God. It was not the result of your own efforts, so you cannot brag about it." Grace is all we need, and we should rejoice!

Yet many of us, including those of us who have already accepted Christ as our Savior, live empty lives because we continue to pursue salvation through our works. But works are a reflection of salvation, not the payment for it. As pastor and author Charles R. Swindoll says in his book *The Grace Awakening*, "Grace received but unexpressed is dead grace. To spend one's time debating how grace is received or how much commitment is necessary for salvation, without getting into what it means to live by grace and enjoy the magnificent freedom it provides, quickly leads to a counterproductive argument. It becomes little more than another tedious trivial pursuit where the majority of God's people spend days looking back and asking, 'How did we receive it?' instead of looking ahead and announcing, 'Grace is ours...let's live it!'"

While some balk at the idea of preaching grace, afraid that those who hear of it will abuse it, we all need to realize that grace is the only way we can gain eternal life in heaven with God. Instead of existing according to a list of do's and don'ts, judging ourselves and others who don't "fall in line" with our expectations, we need to free ourselves and others to live out our relationships with Jesus Christ however he calls us to, knowing that he will only call us to purity in him.

As we embrace this truth, how will it affect our lives? Swindoll gives us four practical expectations:

1. We'll gain a greater appreciation for God's gifts to us,
2. We'll spend less time and energy being critical of and concerned about others' choices,
3. We'll become more tolerant and less judgmental, and
4. We'll take giant steps toward maturity.

(Charles R. Swindoll, *The Grace Awakening*)

So let's live by grace and invite our young people to do the same. In doing so, we'll all enjoy the abundant life Christ promised to those who trust in him.

Give each student a balloon without holes poked in it. Say: **Read John 1:14, 16-17 and Philippians 3:7-9. Then inflate your new balloon, tie it off, and on it, write all the things you find in the Bible passages about how you can have a full life. When you're done, compare notes with the other members of your group and, if you wish, add some of their input to your balloon. Make sure you leave some room to write on your balloon later in the study, and keep your balloon inflated during this activity.**

When groups have finished their Bible discussions, have them discuss these questions:

● **Was it easier to keep your new balloon inflated than your old one? Why or why not?**

● **How was keeping this balloon inflated like finding fulfillment in the things you wrote on this balloon? How was it different?**

● **What was Paul's opinion in Philippians 3:7-9 about the things he trusted to give him a fulfilled life? about trusting in Jesus to give him a fulfilled life?**

● **How does Paul's opinion affect your own? Explain.**

● **What part does Jesus play in leading a full life? What part does grace play?**

● **Have you personally experienced the life fulfillment Jesus offers? Explain.**

● **What could you do this week to find true fulfillment?**

Say: **We all want to lead full lives. We all want to know that our lives fulfill some purpose and have some meaning. As we could see with our first balloons, life is empty without Jesus. No matter what we use to try to fill ourselves up, we leak! So we have to keep trying new things over and over to fill ourselves. But we can never succeed on our own. Yet, as we discovered through the Bible passages, when we trust our lives to Jesus Christ, accepting his gift of grace, he fills our lives with his love and purpose. Let's explore this a little further.**

Have students set their balloons aside for later use.

LEADER TIP for The Study

This study may raise some questions for students about grace. Be prepared to spend some extra time after class or during the week talking with students about how they can receive God's gift of grace and how they can rely on Jesus to fulfill their lives. Make sure you can clearly articulate to them how they can become Christians.

OBJECT LESSON 2 ▼

Drippley's Believe It or Not (20 to 25 minutes) Have students form their original pairs, and hand each pair a paper cup filled with water, two squares of cheesecloth, a rubber band, and a bottle or jar. Ask: **How much faith do you have in the cheesecloth's ability to hold water in your jar or bottle?**

Allow kids to respond. Then say: **Well, we're going to test it. With your partner, pour the water from your paper cup into your jar or bottle. Then cover the mouth of your jar or bottle with both squares of cheesecloth, and put the rubber band around the opening of the jar or bottle, pulling the cheesecloth taut. Then when you're ready, turn over your jar or bottle so its mouth is parallel to the floor. Do this over your paper cup, in case water spills.**

After each group has finished its experiment, have kids turn their bottles and jars right side up again. Have them do this over their paper cups to protect against any spills. Then have pairs return to their foursomes to discuss these questions:

● **What's one thing you enjoyed about doing this project with your partner?**

● **How much faith did you have in the cheesecloth's ability to hold the water? Why?**

LEADER TIP for Drippley's Believe It or Not

If you're a little strapped for time when preparing for this study, just gather one bottle or jar for every four students and cut two squares of cheesecloth for every four students. Have foursomes instead of pairs complete this activity together. Then when each student needs a piece of cheesecloth, set out some scissors and have each pair take a piece of cheesecloth and cut it in half so each student can have a piece.

Running on Empty 41

LEADER TIP
for Drippley's Believe It or Not

During this activity, some water will spill through the cheesecloth as kids turn their bottles over. This will stop once they have their bottles or jars completely parallel to the floor. Because of this, kids may say that this activity couldn't be like Jesus completely fulfilling our lives. If so, you can mention that sometimes when we know Jesus, we still don't trust him fully. Instead we continue to rely on other things to fulfill us. In doing so, we may still experience some "draining" from our lives until we learn to completely trust Jesus.

DEPTH FINDER
UNDERSTANDING OUR EMPTINESS

Why can we say with such certainty that life is empty without Jesus? Many in our culture today would fight that notion, saying that people can find fulfillment in many ways. We can't, these people would say, definitively proclaim one way to be fulfilled. But whatever our society says, we can't deny the truth. And the truth is that we all need Jesus Christ. He said it himself—he's *the* way, *the* truth, and *the* life (John 14:6).

Some have described the emptiness we feel as a God-shaped vacuum. In the book *A Generation Alone*, Janet Bernardi calls it the "God space" and describes it this way:

In every human being there is a space inside for spirituality. This shape is the same for every person and is present in a very clear form from birth. It is...so large that many people cannot define it or see it is there. People for ages have attempted to fill this gaping emptiness with careers, alcohol, other people, drugs, activities or hobbies. Trying to fill the God space with such things is like tossing goldfish into the mouth of a whale. Only God can fill the God space. When we invite God into our space, we find the meaning of life. Literally. And a person cannot be truly fulfilled or truly complete until the God space is occupied.

As our society has continued to deny God's existence, we've seen the rise of overindulgence and addiction. People desperate to feel whole cram their lives with activity, alcohol, drugs, food, sex, exercise, and many other seductive habits. And Christians are not excluded. We all struggle with attempting to fill our lives with everything but Jesus Christ. But as we choose to actively pursue Christ and his gift of grace, we find we don't need those other things as much. Our need for them tapers off until they no longer have a hold on us. Instead, we allow Jesus to take complete control of our lives. Only he can completely fulfill the God space within each of us.

This truth impacts our lives today and forever. We eternally reap the benefits of living by this truth. Neil T. Anderson, counselor and author of *The Bondage Breaker*, puts it like this: "If you want to save your natural life (i.e., find your identity and sense of self-worth in positions, titles, accomplishments, and possessions, and seek only worldly well-being), you will lose it. At best you can only possess these temporal values for a lifetime, only to lose everything for eternity. Furthermore, in all your efforts to possess these earthly treasures, you will fail to gain all that can be yours in Christ. Shoot for this world and that's all you'll get, and eventually you will lose even that. But shoot for the next world and God will throw in this one as a bonus." Accept and live by God's gift of grace through Jesus Christ, and you'll have life to the fullest both in this life and the next.

● How did your level of faith compare to the reality you saw when you actually turned over your jar or bottle?

● How was your level of faith in the cheesecloth's ability to hold the water like your level of faith in Jesus' ability to fulfill you? Why?

● Read Ephesians 2:4-9 and Philippians 3:10-11. What do these passages say about how Jesus can give us fulfilling lives? What part does grace play in this?

When groups have finished their discussions, invite students to share their insights with the rest of the class. Then give each person a short strip of tape and a marker. Encourage each student to take a piece of cheesecloth from his or her experiment, tape it to his or her balloon from "The Bottomless Balloon" activity, and write a statement about his or her faith in Jesus Christ to fulfill his or her life. Then say: **Life is empty without Jesus.** **We've seen it in our activities today, we've seen it in the Bible passages we've explored, and we've seen it in the lives of people we know. Perhaps we've even seen it in our own lives. But when we trust Jesus Christ with our lives, we experience a fulfillment we could never imagine otherwise.**

The wonderful thing about experiencing abundant life is that we can do nothing to earn it. It's a gift from God. By his grace, he has made a way for us to experience it—through the death and resurrection of his Son, Jesus Christ. When we accept this gift, God gives us the fullest life imaginable for all eternity.

Read aloud Romans 8:10-13. Then say: **Let's look at life in three phases: the life you've led up until today, the life you'll lead from this moment on, and the life that can be yours after death. For a moment, think of each of these phases in your life. How fulfilled have you been? How fulfilled will you be? What part will Jesus play in your future fulfillment, especially in the eternal life that comes after this life? Write your responses on your balloon.**

If students don't have any more room to write on their balloons, offer them sheets of paper. If they wish, they can tape their sheets of paper to their balloons.

Invite students to share what they wrote with their foursomes if they wish. Then have foursomes pray for each other that they might experience God's grace through Jesus Christ and in doing so experience truly fulfilling lives. Have kids take home their balloons as reminders that they can find fulfillment only in Jesus.

LEADER TIP for Drippley's Believe It or Not

This activity involves water, and in the process of completing the task, your students may spill some of the water. So make any necessary precautions to maintain the cleanliness of your classroom! Lay a tarp down over the floor in one area of the room, and have groups complete the task over the tarp. Or bring in a few buckets, and have groups complete the task over the buckets.

THE ISSUE: Faith

Like A Child

by Lisa Baba Lauffer

HELPING YOUNG PEOPLE UNDERSTAND HOW TO TRUST GOD COMPLETELY

■ "Mo-o-ommy! Da-a-addy!" ■ Perhaps you remember those days of lying awake at night, afraid of the monsters under the bed or the boogeyman in the closet. Perhaps you cried for Mommy or Daddy in the night, and you remember the sense of relief you felt when she or he heard your cry, came to you, and comforted you. Suddenly your fears disintegrated into the very darkness that evoked them. ■ Your young people

THE POINT:

Faith is simple trust in God.

are at the stage in life when they're forsaking the need for Mommy and Daddy in the night and embracing independence with everything they have. Yet as fun as growing up can be, it also evokes insecurity and fear. Will they make it? Will they see their way through all the obstacles that present themselves along the way? And, in the end, will they have secured their salvation? ■ As we grow, the world gets even scarier than monsters and boogeymen, yet because we value independence, we feel the need to face these "grown-up" fears alone. But we don't have to, not even when we're facing the deepest darkness we'll ever encounter—death. If we can once again embrace that childlike trust, crying for our Father in the night, he'll see us safely home for now and eternity. ■ This study will challenge your young people to see their need for a heavenly Father who they can trust with their lives. And it will show them how to trust God with faith like a child.

The Study
AT A GLANCE

SECTION	MINUTES	WHAT STUDENTS WILL DO	SUPPLIES
Childlike Experiences	10 to 15	HOW TO EAT LIKE A CHILD—Develop and demonstrate creative ways that children eat food.	Slips of paper, pencils, assorted office and home supplies
	10 to 15	THE WRITING ON THE WALLS—Respond to questions about their childhood on sheets of newsprint taped to the walls.	Newsprint, tape, crayons
Bible Exploration	15 to 20	ME AND DADDY—Explore God's fatherlike qualities and Jesus' view of children.	Bibles, newsprint, crayons, "Kids Kwotes" handout (p. 53), "Operating Manual" handout (p. 54)
Life Application	10 to 15	LEAVING LIFE IN GOD'S HANDS—Consider ways they can trust God with their toughest problems, then choose one of those ways to put into practice during the week.	Bible, slips of paper from the "How to Eat Like a Child" activity, newsprint from "The Writing on the Walls" activity, crayons

notes:

THE POINT OF *LIKE A CHILD:*
Faith is simple trust in God.

THE BIBLE CONNECTION

DEUTERONOMY 1:31; ISAIAH 43:1-7; MATTHEW 6:31-34	These passages describe some of God's fatherlike qualities.
MATTHEW 11:25-30; 18:1-5; ROMANS 8:14-17; 1 JOHN 3:1-2	These passages exhort us to approach our relationship with Jesus Christ as children would.
ROMANS 1:17	This passage explains that we are made right with God through faith.
HEBREWS 11:1	This passage reveals the nature of faith.

In this study, kids will revert back to childhood by demonstrating how to eat like children and by writing on (paper-covered) walls with crayons. Then they'll explore Scripture passages describing faith, Jesus' view of children, and God's fatherlike qualities.

Through these experiences, kids can discover that they can approach God as children, giving him all their needs—especially their need for eternal life.

Explore the verses in The Bible Connection, then examine the information in the Depthfinder boxes throughout the study to gain a deeper understanding of how these Scriptures connect with your young people.

LEADER TIP for The Study

Whenever groups discuss a list of questions, write the questions on newsprint and tape the newsprint to the wall so groups can discuss the questions at their own pace.

BEFORE THE STUDY

For the "How to Eat Like a Child" activity, collect a variety of office and home supplies you have available such as paper, markers, paper clips, tape, self-stick notes, a stapler and staples, old pantyhose, and anything else that captures your imagination.

For "The Writing on the Walls" activity, tape sheets of newsprint to the walls of your meeting room, making sure that you have at least one sheet for each student. Tape the newsprint sheets at a lower level so your students will have to kneel or sit when writing on them. On the floor beneath the newsprint, scatter assorted colors of crayons.

Like a Child   47

THE STUDY

CHILDLIKE EXPERIENCES ▼

How to Eat Like a Child (10 to 15 minutes) As students arrive, hand each one a slip of paper and a pencil. Have each person write down the most serious problem he or she faces. For example, students might write that their parents are divorcing, that they don't know what to do after high school graduation, or that they don't know how to confront a friend who drinks. Then have kids fold their slips of paper and place them somewhere they can get them later in the study. While kids work, set out the assorted office and home supplies.

When everyone has finished, say: **Today we're going to revert back to childhood. So get ready! One rule we have for today is that we're going to go by the "buddy system." So find a buddy. You'll have to keep track of this person throughout the study.**

When everyone has found a buddy, say: **Having been children at one time, you may well know that children have an interesting relationship with food. Quite often, children find creative ways to eat all different kinds of food. So in your pairs, I want you to demonstrate how to eat like a child. You can do this with any food you wish: a favorite food from childhood, a food you've recently seen a child eat creatively, or anything else that sparks your imagination. Have one partner use the supplies I've provided to demonstrate how to eat your chosen food like a child, and have the other partner narrate the process to the class. For example, one partner could take a sheet of paper, roll it up, and demonstrate how to eat a Hostess Ho Ho by pretending to nibble off the chocolate coating, unroll the Ho Ho, lick out the cream filling, fold the chocolate-cake layer, and leave the folded chocolate cake on a table. While one partner demonstrates how to eat like a child, the other partner must give blow-by-blow coverage of the process. You have five minutes to brainstorm.**

After five minutes, have pairs demonstrate their chosen ways to eat like children. Then have buddies find another pair of buddies to discuss these questions:

● **What's your response to this activity?**
● **How was this activity like being a child? How was it different?**
● **Did this activity help you tap into your own childhood? Why or why not?**
● **What were some really cool things about being a child?**
● **What was one fun thing about doing this activity with your buddy?**

When groups have finished their discussions, invite students to share any of their answers to the questions. Then say: **In its purest**

LEADER TIP for How to Eat Like a Child

For added fun, provide actual food items and have each pair demonstrate how to eat like a child with one of the provided items. Assign a different item to each pair. Good foods for this activity are french fries, spaghetti, ice cream cones, ice cream sandwiches, peanut butter and jelly sandwiches, peas, bananas, and anything else that you've observed kids eat in a creative way.

Like a Child 48

DEPTHFINDER: UNDERSTANDING THE BIBLE

To place simple, childlike faith in God, we have to understand that he is our Father in heaven. Here are some Scripture passages that describe a few of God's fatherly characteristics:

- Psalm 103:13—He has mercy on us.
- Isaiah 64:8—He created us.
- Jeremiah 31:20—He loves us and wants to comfort us.
- Matthew 6:6—He rewards the good things we do in secret.
- Matthew 7:11—He gives good things to those who ask him.
- Hebrews 12:5-6—He disciplines us.
- 1 Peter 1:17—He judges each of us equally, and he is worthy of our respect.

If any of your students would like to do further exploration about how God is a father, give them photocopies of this Depthfinder and encourage them to study the passages listed.

Permission to photocopy this Depthfinder from Group's Core Belief Bible Study Series granted for local church use. Copyright © Group Publishing, Inc., P.O. Box 481, Loveland, CO 80539.

LEADER TIP for The Study

Because this topic can be so powerful and relevant to kids' lives, your group members may be tempted to get caught up in issues and lose sight of the deeper biblical principle found in The Point. Help your kids grasp The Point by guiding them to focus on the biblical investigation and discussing how God's truth connects with reality in their lives.

sense, childhood is a time for wonder, for growing, for trusting in others to take care of each and every one of our needs. Today we'll discuss how Jesus wants us to come to him like children; when we have childlike faith in him, he'll take care of all our needs, for <u>faith is simple trust in God.</u>

Before we move on to a more in-depth discussion of this truth, let's get a little more in touch with our own childhood.

Hebrews 12: 5-6

You have forgotten the encouraging words that call you his children: "My child, don't think the Lord's discipline is worth nothing, and don't stop trying when he corrects you. **The Lord disciplines those he loves, and he punishes everyone he accepts as his child."**

The Writing on the Walls (10 to 15 minutes)

Have each student go to a sheet of newsprint taped to a wall. Say: **Think of the best period of time in your childhood. Maybe it was when you were six and went to school for the first time. Perhaps you remember a special vacation to a relative's farm when you were nine years old. Whatever age you choose, take a moment to remember what being that age was like.**

Pause for students to reflect and then say: **I'm going to ask you a few questions about being a child. Answer these questions as if you are**

Like a Child 49

LEADER TIP for The Study

Your students may want to know more about how they can have faith in God. Be prepared to answer questions after the study about how to gain eternal life by trusting in Jesus Christ.

DEPTHFINDER — UNDERSTANDING FAITH

The author of Hebrews says "Faith means being sure of the things we hope for and knowing that something is real even if we do not see it" (Hebrews 11:1). But faith is a difficult concept to define and an even more difficult reality to pursue. Perhaps that is why we need to be like children to truly have it. Children believe in so many things just because someone tells them to. They take things at face value. If their trust hasn't been breached, they trust in people to be there for them whenever they have a need.

Yet as we grow older and pursue independence and learn to rely on ourselves to fulfill our own needs, we lose that sense of the wonder of life and that ability to trust wholly. Your young people are at this point right now. What we all need to do is to learn to keep one foot in that world of wonder by trusting in God to see us through each day. As we hand even our simplest problems to him and watch him come through 100 percent of the time, that childlike ability to completely trust another reawakens. And recovering that sense is essential, because in this simple yet profound truth comes our deepest healing and ultimately our source of eternal life—childlike trust in Jesus Christ to fulfill his promise and take us home.

your favorite age from childhood. **Using crayons, write or draw your answers to the questions on the newsprint in front of you. Use your weak hand to write or draw (if you're right-handed, write with your left hand, and vice versa).** Ask each of the following questions, allowing time between questions for kids to write or draw their answers:

● **How old are you?**
● **What's the best thing about being your age?**
● **Who is the person you trust the most?**
● **What makes that person so trustworthy?**
● **What are your biggest needs right now?**
● **What do you believe about God?**

Say: **Now write or draw a prayer to God about whatever you need to talk to him about. Maybe you have a deep need, or perhaps you just want to thank him for your favorite animal or flower.**

After a moment, say: **Now find your buddy, and share with your buddy what you wrote and drew on your sheet of newsprint.** When buddies have finished sharing, have each pair meet with another pair of buddies (not necessarily the same pair from the first activity) to discuss these questions:

● **What were you thinking and feeling as you got into the mind-set of a child?**
● **How did it feel to write with your weak hand? to write in crayon? How were those activities like being a child? How were they different?**
● **Do you have any needs today that are similar to the needs you had as a child? If so, what?**
● **How do you go about getting your needs met now that you're a teenager and approaching adulthood?**
● **What are some areas of your life that you wish you could**

Like a Child 50

give over to someone else? Are there any ways that God can take care of those areas? Explain.

When groups have finished their discussions, say: **There are so many cool things about growing older—driving, dating, leading your life on your own terms, making life decisions. Yet growing up can also be scary, and as we grow older we often feel like the world is on our shoulders. But God tells us that we can come to him like children, and he'll take care of us. All we have to do is place our <u>faith—our simple trust—in him.</u>**

BIBLE EXPLORATION ▼

Me and Daddy (15 to 20 minutes)

Say: **I've talked a bit already about faith. So before we go much further, let's figure out what faith is.** Read aloud Hebrews 11:1, and have students volunteer their insights about and examples of faith. Then say: **In a moment, we're going to do a little more in-depth study about how to have faith in God. But before we do, let's pray that God will show us what faith means and how to have this simple trust in him.** Offer a short prayer asking God to reveal what he will about faith and about how to trust him as children trust the adults around them.

Then have students form two groups by having buddies in each pair go to opposite sides of the room. Give both groups Bibles, newsprint, and crayons. Give one group a copy of the "Kids Kwotes" handout (p. 53), and give the other group a copy of the "Operating Manual" handout (p. 54). Direct groups to go through their handouts, completing the tasks described and discussing the questions listed.

When groups have finished going through their handouts, have buddies find each other and share with each other the sentences their groups brainstormed. Then encourage them to share any other insights they gained through their group discussions.

Then say: **As you've collaborated with your buddy, you've come up with a rounded picture of <u>faith as simple, childlike trust in our heavenly Father.</u> In a minute, we'll talk about how to make what you've learned a little more personal.**

LIFE APPLICATION ▼

Leaving Life in God's Hands (10 to 15 minutes)

Have students retrieve their slips of paper from the first activity. Say: **With your buddy, brainstorm ways you can trust God with your problem.** Give pairs a couple of minutes to discuss this, then invite students to tell the rest of the class ways they can trust God through their issues. Then say: **We can place simple trust in God for any problem that comes our way. He is our Father who cares for us. In fact, he cares so much for us that he figured out**

LEADER TIP for Me and Daddy

If you have access to a children's Sunday school class or another children's gathering while you're doing this study, ask the leader ahead of time if your students can interview some of the children. Then, instead of having one group use the quotes on the "Kids Kwotes" handout (p. 53), have the group interview kids asking questions such as "What do you believe about God?" Then have this group go through the rest of the "Kids Kwotes" handout (p. 53), using the information they gained through their interviews. You might want to provide kids with paper and pencils to record the children's responses.

LEADER TIP for Me and Daddy

If you have more than eight students in each of the two groups, have kids find partners within their groups. Hand each pair a copy of their group's handout, and have kids do the activities and discuss the questions in their pairs.

Like a Child 51

LEADER TIP for The Study

To add to the discussion, play the Jars of Clay song called "Like a Child" from their *Jars of Clay* album. Then have kids discuss what the song says about faith—what faith is, how to have it, what it's like to live without it, and any other insights they may have.

a way for us to solve our most deadly problem: our sinfulness.

Read aloud Romans 1:17, then say: **In this passage, the Apostle Paul says that God makes us righteous through our faith, and that means that we can live forever with God in his presence. There's nothing difficult about this process; <u>faith is simple trust in God.</u>**

Direct kids to return to their spaces by the wall. Say: **Some of you may need to cultivate simple faith today either for the problem you wrote down at the beginning of this study or maybe for an eternal relationship with God. On your section of newsprint, if you choose, write one way you will place simple, childlike faith in God this week.**

When kids have finished writing, encourage them to tear from their newsprint what they just wrote and take it home as a reminder to trust in God during the week. If they wish, let kids take their entire sheets of newsprint home.

DEPTHFINDER — UNDERSTANDING TODAY'S KIDS

Adolescence is a natural time when young people leave childhood behind and transition into adulthood. For many, this is a change they embrace. They look forward to new independence, making their own choices and having no one to answer to. Others mourn this change, wishing they could stay in the protective relationship under their parents' wings. Most vacillate between these two reactions, asserting their own identities one minute and clinging to Mom or Dad the next.

However, our society has seen a disturbing trend over the past couple of decades. This trend can best be characterized by the title of a popular book: *The Hurried Child* by David Elkind. Elkind contends that our culture has expected too much of children, hurrying them to embrace adult roles that they are ill-equipped to fulfill.

Hurried children are forced to take on the physical, psychological, and social trappings of adulthood before they are prepared to deal with them. We dress our children in miniature adult costumes (often with designer labels), we expose them to gratuitous sex and violence, and we expect them to cope with an increasingly bewildering social environment—divorce, single parenthood, homosexuality. Through all of these pressures the child senses that it is important for him or her to cope without admitting the confusion and pain that accompany such changes. Like adults, they are made to feel they must be survivors, and surviving means adjusting—even if the survivor is only four or six or eight years old. This pressure to cope without cracking is a stress in itself, the effect of which must be tallied with all the other effects of hurrying our children.

Having endured these kinds of influences and expectations, many of today's teenagers balk at the idea of placing simple trust in anyone, least of all a father figure. Many don't know how to be children, having been the adult in the family for so long. And yet deep down, they have a need for guidance, comfort, nurturing, and selfless love.

This is the very reason that young people need to trust their heavenly Father. They don't need to run their own lives anymore; God will show them the way when they place their lives in his strong, able hands.

Like a Child 52

Kids "Kwotes"

Read the following quotes from kids about God. Then, on your sheet of newsprint, have a volunteer list the things you observe from these quotes about children's faith in God. Add to your list anything you've observed in kids about how they trust God simply.

"God is the kings of heaven, and Jesus."—Curtis, 4

"You want to know what lightning **really** is? It's God turning on and off a night light."—Acacia, 4

"God is purple."—Kaylee, 3

"God can do anything!"—Tony, 6 1/2

"That's not it, Daddy. Wind *is* God and Jesus breathing." —Adrienne, 4 1/2

Now have someone in your group read aloud Matthew 11:25-30; 18:1-5; Romans 8:14-17; and 1 John 3:1-2. Then, as a group, brainstorm all the things these passages say about trusting God like a child. Have a volunteer write all your ideas on the newsprint.

After you've completed your list, discuss these questions:
- What was Jesus' view of children?
- What do these verses say about how we're supposed to trust in God like children?
- How do these passages show us that faith is simple trust in God?
- How do the quotes you read earlier show how children trust God?
- What are some things we can trust God for as children trust?

Now, having studied the quotes and the Bible passages about trusting in God like a child, brainstorm your own quote that expresses childlike faith in God. Make sure it fully and accurately describes how you can trust in God. Commit it to memory, because you'll share it with your buddy when you reunite with him or her.

Permission to photocopy this handout from Group's Core Belief Bible Study Series granted for local church use.
Copyright © Group Publishing, Inc., P.O. Box 481, Loveland, CO 80539.

Operating Manual

A ←——————————→ B

As a group, create an Operating Manual for children. In this manual, include all the things parents need to do to properly raise children. Be as thorough as possible. Have a volunteer write all your responses on the newsprint.

When you've finished, discuss these questions:

- When you were a child, who most often fulfilled the responsibilities you've listed on the newsprint?
- How fully did that person fulfill those responsibilities? Explain.
- What was one time that an adult disappointed you by not meeting a specific need you had? How did you respond?
- What would you say if you could meet and know a Father who would never let you down and would meet each and every one of your needs?

Have each of three volunteers in your group read aloud one of the following passages: Deuteronomy 1:31; Isaiah 43:1-7; and Matthew 6:31-34. Then list all the things these passages say about how God is a Father whom you can trust for every one of your needs. Have a volunteer write your responses on the newsprint.

When you've finished, discuss these questions:

- Looking at the list you've created, how do you feel knowing that God is a Father who will meet all your needs?
- How well would God fulfill all the responsibilities listed in your Operating Manual?
- What kinds of needs do people have today that they can find fulfilled in God the Father?
- Do you trust God to care for all your needs? Why or why not?

Now, come up with one sentence that describes how God is a Father you can trust for everything. Make sure it is something you can remember, because you'll share it with your buddy soon.

Permission to photocopy this handout from Group's Core Belief Bible Study Series granted for local church use.
Copyright © Group Publishing, Inc., P.O. Box 481, Loveland, CO 80539.

why Active and Interactive Learning works with teenagers

Let's Start With the Big Picture

Think back to a major life lesson you've learned.
Got it? Now answer these questions:
- Did you learn your lesson from something you read?
- Did you learn it from something you heard?
- Did you learn it from something you experienced?

If you're like 99 percent of your peers, you answered "yes" only to the third question—you learned your life lesson from something you experienced.

This simple test illustrates the most convincing reason for using active and interactive learning with young people: People learn best through experience. Or to put it even more simply, people learn by doing.

Learning by doing is what active learning is all about. No more sitting quietly in chairs and listening to a speaker expound theories about God—that's passive learning. Active learning gets kids out of their chairs and into the experience of life. With active learning, kids get to *do* what they're studying. They *feel* the effects of the principles you teach. They *learn* by experiencing truth firsthand.

Active learning works because it recognizes three basic learning needs and uses them in concert to enable young people to make discoveries on their own and to find practical life applications for the truths they believe.

So what are these three basic learning needs?
1. Teenagers need action.
2. Teenagers need to think.
3. Teenagers need to talk.

Read on to find out exactly how these needs will be met by using the active and interactive learning techniques in Group's Core Belief Bible Study Series in your youth group.

1. Teenagers Need Action

Aircraft pilots know well the difference between passive and active learning. Their passive learning comes through listening to flight instructors and reading flight-instruction books. Their active learning comes through actually flying an airplane or flight simulator. Books and lectures may be helpful, but pilots really learn to fly by manipulating a plane's controls themselves.

We can help young people learn in a similar way. Though we may engage students passively in some reading and listening to teachers, their understanding and application of God's Word will really take off through simulated and real-life experiences.

Forms of active learning include simulation games; role-plays; service projects; experiments; research projects; group pantomimes; mock trials; construction projects; purposeful games; field trips; and, of course, the most powerful form of active learning—real-life experiences.

We can more fully explain active learning by exploring four of its characteristics:

● **Active learning is an adventure.** Passive learning is almost always predictable. Students sit passively while the teacher or speaker follows a planned outline or script.

In active learning, kids may learn lessons the teacher never envisioned. Because the leader trusts students to help create the learning experience, learners may venture into unforeseen discoveries. And often the teacher learns as much as the students.

● **Active learning is fun and captivating.** What are we communicating when we say, "OK, the fun's over—time to talk about God"? What's the hidden message? That joy is separate from God? And that learning is separate from joy?

What a shame.

Active learning is not joyless. One seventh-grader we interviewed clearly remembered her best Sunday school lesson: "Jesus was the light, and we went into a dark room and shut off the lights. We had a candle, and we learned that Jesus is the light and the dark can't shut off the light." That's active learning. Deena enjoyed the lesson. She had fun. And she learned.

Active learning intrigues people. Whether they find a foot-washing experience captivating or maybe a bit uncomfortable, they learn. And they learn on a level deeper than any work sheet or teacher's lecture could ever reach.

● **Active learning involves everyone.** Here the difference between passive and active learning becomes abundantly clear. It's like the difference between watching a football game on television and actually playing in the game.

The "trust walk" provides a good example of involving everyone in active learning. Half of the group members put on blindfolds; the other half serve as guides. The "blind" people trust the guides to lead them through the building or outdoors. The guides prevent the blind people from falling down stairs or tripping over rocks. Everyone needs to participate to learn the inherent lessons of trust, faith, doubt, fear, confidence, and servanthood. Passive spectators of this experience would learn little, but participants learn a great deal.

● **Active learning is focused through debriefing.** Activity simply for activity's sake doesn't usually result in good learning. Debriefing—evaluating an experience by discussing it in pairs or small groups—helps focus the experience and draw out its meaning. Debriefing helps sort and order the information students gather during the experience. It helps learners relate the recently experienced activity to their lives.

The process of debriefing is best started immediately after an experience. We use a three-step process in debriefing: reflection, interpretation, and application.

Reflection—This first step asks the students, "How did you feel?" Active-learning experiences typically evoke an emotional reaction, so it's appropriate to begin debriefing at that level.

Some people ask, "What do feelings have to do with education?" Feelings have everything to do with education. Think back again to that time in your life when you learned a big lesson. In all likelihood, strong feelings accompanied that lesson. Our emotions tend to cement things into our memories.

When you're debriefing, use open-ended questions to probe feelings. Avoid questions that can be answered with a "yes" or "no." Let your learners know that there are no wrong answers to these "feeling" questions. Everyone's feelings are valid.

Interpretation—The next step in the debriefing process asks, "What does this mean to you? How is this experience like or unlike some other aspect of your life?" Now you're asking people to identify a message or principle from the experience.

You want your learners to discover the message for themselves. So instead of telling students your answers, take the time to ask questions that encourage self-discovery. Use Scripture and discussion in pairs or small groups to explore how the actions and effects of the activity might translate to their lives.

Alert! Some of your people may interpret wonderful messages that you never intended. That's not failure! That's the Holy Spirit at work. God allows us to catch different glimpses of his kingdom even when we all look through the same glass.

Application—The final debriefing step asks, "What will you do about it?" This step moves learning into action. Your young people have shared a common experience. They've discovered a principle. Now they must create something new with what they've just experienced and interpreted. They must integrate the message into their lives.

The application stage of debriefing calls for a decision. Ask your students how they'll change, how they'll grow, what they'll do as a result of your time together.

2. Teenagers Need to Think

Today's students have been trained not to think. They aren't dumber than previous generations. We've simply conditioned them not to use their heads.

You see, we've trained our kids to respond with the simplistic answers they think the teacher wants to hear. Fill-in-the-blank student workbooks and teachers who ask dead-end questions such as "What's the capital of Delaware?" have produced kids and adults who have learned not to think.

And it doesn't just happen in junior high or high school. Our children are schooled very early not to think. Teachers attempt to help kids read with nonsensical fill-in-the-blank drills, word scrambles, and missing-letter puzzles.

Helping teenagers think requires a paradigm shift in how we teach. We need to plan for and set aside time for higher-order thinking and be willing to reduce our time spent on lower-order parroting. Group's Core Belief Bible Study Series is designed to help you do just that.

Thinking classrooms look quite different from traditional classrooms. In most church environments, the teacher does most of the talking and hopes that knowledge will transmit from his or her brain to the students'. In thinking settings, the teacher coaches students to ponder, wonder, imagine, and problem-solve.

3. Teenagers Need to Talk

Everyone knows that the person who learns the most in any class is the teacher. Explaining a concept to someone else is usually more helpful to the explainer than to the listener. So why not let the students do more teaching? That's one of the chief benefits of letting kids do the talking. This process is called interactive learning.

What is interactive learning? Interactive learning occurs when students discuss and work cooperatively in pairs or small groups.

Interactive learning encourages learners to work together. It honors the fact that students can learn from one another, not just from the teacher. Students work together in pairs or small groups to accomplish shared goals. They build together, discuss together, and present together. They teach each other and learn from one another. Success as a group is celebrated. Positive interdependence promotes individual and group learning.

Interactive learning not only helps people learn but also helps learners feel better about themselves and get along better with others. It accomplishes these things more effectively than the independent or competitive methods.

Here's a selection of interactive learning techniques that are used in Group's Core Belief Bible Study Series. With any of these models, leaders may assign students to specific partners or small groups. This will maximize cooperation and learning by preventing all the "rowdies" from linking up. And it will allow for new friendships to form outside of established cliques.

Following any period of partner or small-group work, the leader may reconvene the entire class for large-group processing. During this time the teacher may ask for reports or discoveries from individuals or teams. This technique builds in accountability for the teacherless pairs and small groups.

Pair-Share—With this technique each student turns to a partner and responds to a question or problem from the teacher or leader. Every learner responds. There are no passive observers. The teacher may then ask people to share their partners' responses.

Study Partners—Most curricula and most teachers call for Scripture passages to be read to the whole class by one person. One reads; the others doze.

Why not relinquish some teacher control and let partners read and react with each other? They'll all be involved—and will learn more.

Learning Groups—Students work together in small groups to create a model, design artwork, or study a passage or story; then they discuss what they learned through the experience. Each person in the learning group may be assigned a specific role. Here are some examples:

Reader

Recorder (makes notes of key thoughts expressed during the reading or discussion)

Checker (makes sure everyone understands and agrees with answers arrived at by the group)

Encourager (urges silent members to share their thoughts)

When everyone has a specific responsibility, knows what it is, and contributes to a small group, much is accomplished and much is learned.

Summary Partners—One student reads a paragraph, then the partner summarizes the paragraph or interprets its meaning. Partners alternate roles with each paragraph.

The paraphrasing technique also works well in discussions. Anyone who wishes to share a thought must first paraphrase what the previous person said. This sharpens listening skills and demonstrates the power of feedback communication.

Jigsaw—Each person in a small group examines a different concept, Scripture, or part of an issue. Then each teaches the others in the group. Thus, all members teach, and all must learn the others' discoveries. This technique is called a jigsaw because individuals are responsible to their group for different pieces of the puzzle.

JIGSAW EXAMPLE

Here's an example of a jigsaw.

Assign four-person teams. Have teammates each number off from one to four. Have all the Ones go to one corner of the room, all the Twos to another corner, and so on.

Tell team members they're responsible for learning information in their numbered corners and then for teaching their team members when they return to their original teams.

Give the following assignments to various groups:

Ones: Read Psalm 22. Discuss and list the prophecies made about Jesus.

Twos: Read Isaiah 52:13–53:12. Discuss and list the prophecies made about Jesus.

Threes: Read Matthew 27:1-32. Discuss and list the things that happened to Jesus.

Fours: Read Matthew 27:33-66. Discuss and list the things that happened to Jesus.

After the corner groups meet and discuss, instruct all learners to return to their original teams and report what they've learned. Then have each team determine which prophecies about Jesus were fulfilled in the passages from Matthew.

Call on various individuals in each team to report one or two prophecies that were fulfilled.

You Can Do It Too!

All this information may sound revolutionary to you, but it's really not. God has been using active and interactive learning to teach his people for generations. Just look at Abraham and Isaac, Jacob and Esau, Moses and the Israelites, Ruth and Boaz. And then there's Jesus, who used active learning all the time!

Group's Core Belief Bible Study Series makes it easy for you to use active and interactive learning with your group. The active and interactive elements are automatically built in! Just follow the outlines, and watch as your kids grow through experience and positive interaction with others.

FOR DEEPER STUDY

For more information on incorporating active and interactive learning into your work with teenagers, check out these resources:

● *Why Nobody Learns Much of Anything at Church: And How to Fix It,* by Thom and Joani Schultz (Group Publishing) and

● *Do It! Active Learning in Youth Ministry,* by Thom and Joani Schultz (Group Publishing).

your evaluation of

Bible Study Series
for senior high

why BEING A CHRISTIAN matters

Group Publishing, Inc.
Attention: Core Belief Talk-back
P.O. Box 481
Loveland, CO 80539
Fax: (970) 669-1994

Please help us continue to provide innovative and useful resources for ministry. After you've led the studies in this volume, take a moment to fill out this evaluation; then mail or fax it to us at the address above. Thanks!

• • • • • •

1. As a whole, this book has been (circle one)

not very helpful   very helpful
1   2   3   4   5   6   7   8   9   10

2. The best things about this book:

3. How this book could be improved:

4. What I will change because of this book:

5. Would you be interested in field-testing future Core Belief Bible Studies and giving us your feedback? If so, please complete the information below:

Name _____

Street address _____

City _____ State _____ Zip _____

Daytime telephone (____) _____ Date _____

THANKS!

Permission to photocopy this evaluation from Group's Core Belief Bible Study Series granted for local church use.
Copyright © Group Publishing, Inc., P.O. Box 481, Loveland, CO 80539.

Give Your Teenagers a Solid Faith Foundation That Lasts a Lifetime!

Here are the *essentials* of the Christian life—core values teenagers *must* believe to make good decisions now...and build an *unshakable* lifelong faith. Developed by youth workers like you...field-tested with *real* youth groups in *real* churches...here's the meat your kids *must* have to grow spiritually—presented in a fun, involving way!

Each 4-session, **Core Belief Bible Study Series** book lets you easily...

- Lead deep, compelling, *relevant* discussions your kids won't want to miss...
- Involve teenagers in exploring life-changing truths...
- Ground your teenagers in God's Word...and
- Help kids create healthy relationships with each other—and you!
- **Plus you'll make an *eternal difference* in the lives of your kids** as you give them a solid faith foundation that stands firm on God's Word—with Group's **Core Belief Bible Study Series!**

Core Belief Bible Study Series lessons are flexible...and simple, step-by-step directions make leading your group easy whether you're a veteran youth worker or a first-time volunteer! Pick and choose which core beliefs your teenagers most need to explore! Each 4-session book is all you need for any size group!

Here are the Core Belief Bible Study Series titles already available...

Senior High Studies

Why **Being a Christian** Matters	ISBN 0-7644-0883-6
Why **God** Matters	ISBN 0-7644-0874-7
Why **Jesus Christ** Matters	ISBN 0-7644-0875-5
Why **Suffering** Matters	ISBN 0-7644-0879-8
Why the **Bible** Matters	ISBN 0-7644-0882-8
Why the **Holy Spirit** Matters	ISBN 0-7644-0876-3

Junior High/Middle School Studies

The Truth About **Being a Christian**	ISBN 0-7644-0859-3
The Truth About **God**	ISBN 0-7644-0850-X
The Truth About **Jesus Christ**	ISBN 0-7644-0851-8
The Truth About **Suffering**	ISBN 0-7644-0855-0
The Truth About the **Bible**	ISBN 0-7644-0858-5
The Truth About the **Holy Spirit**	ISBN 0-7644-0852-6

Order today from your local Christian bookstore, or write: Group Publishing, P.O. Box 485, Loveland, CO 80539.

Practical Resources for Your Youth Ministry

Fun & Rowdy

Here are teenagers' 25 favorite fun and rowdy songs, each complete with quick, on-the-spot activities that involve kids directly in the music and message of each tune.

And whether you play guitar or piano—you're covered! You get both piano accompaniment and guitar chords.

Youth workers, Sunday school teachers, youth worship leaders, and youth choirs will all applaud these most-requested, raise-the-rafters, upbeat songs.

ISBN 1-55945-475-X

Group's Best Discussion Launchers for Youth Ministry

You want your kids to open up. To get past giving you the "right" answers to share what they're *really* thinking and feeling.

No problem. Here's the definitive collection of Group's best-ever discussion launchers!

You'll get **thought-provoking questions** kids can't *resist* answering...**compelling quotes** that *demand* a response...and **quick activities** that pull kids into an experience they can't *wait* to talk about.

Add zing to your youth meetings...revive meetings that are drifting off-track...and comfortably approach sensitive topics like AIDS, war, cults, gangs, suicide, dating, parents, self-image, and more.

ISBN 0-7644-2023-2

You-Choose-the-Ending Skits for Youth Ministry
Stephen Parolini

There's nothing quite as boring as "Sunday school skits" with endings you can see a mile away. Your kids hate them. You hate them. *So quit doing them!*

Instead, try these 19 hot-topic skits *guaranteed* to keep your kids on the edge of their seats—because each skit has **three possible endings!**

You can choose the ending...flip a coin...or let your teenagers vote. No matter which ending you pick, you'll get a great discussion going about a topic kids care about!

Skits require few actors...little or no rehearsal...and many skits get your audience involved, too, for maximum impact. Included: no-fail discussion questions!

ISBN 1-55945-627-2

More Practical Resources for Your Youth Ministry

Last Impressions: Unforgettable Closings for Youth Meetings

Here's a collection of over 170 of Group's best-ever low-prep (or no-prep!) meeting closings...and each is tied to a thought-provoking Bible passage! You'll be ready with thoughtful...affirming...issue-oriented...high-energy...prayerful...and servanthood closings—on a moment's notice!

1-55945-629-9

Ready-to-Use Letters for Youth Ministry

Tom Tozer

These 110 already-written letters cover practically any situation that arises in youth ministry. And the included IBM-compatible computer disk makes adapting these letters quick and easy. You'll save hours of administrative time with this handy resource!

1-55945-692-2

Get Real: Making Core Christian Beliefs Relevant to Teenagers

Mike Nappa, Amy Nappa & Michael D. Warden

Here are the 24 Bible truths that Christian teenagers *must* know to survive in an unbelieving world. Included: proven strategies for effectively communicating these core Christian beliefs into the chaotic, fast-paced youth culture.

1-55945-708-2

Growing Close

These 150 practical, quick ideas help break the ice when teenagers don't know each other and break down cliques that often form in groups. A must-have resource for youth workers, coaches, camp directors, and Christian school teachers.

1-55945-709-0

Order today from your local Christian bookstore, or write: Group Publishing, P.O. Box 485, Loveland, CO 80539.